SMART
THINKING

For
Jane and Verity (as ever)

SMART
THINKING

SKILLS FOR CRITICAL UNDERSTANDING AND WRITING

Second Edition

MATTHEW ALLEN

OXFORD

UNIVERSITY PRESS

OXFORD
UNIVERSITY PRESS

253 Normanby Road, South Melbourne, Victoria 3205, Australia

Oxford University Press is a department of the University of Oxford. It furthers the University's objective of excellence in research, scholarship, and education by publishing worldwide in

Oxford New York

Auckland Bangkok Buenos Aires Cape Town Chennai
Dar es Salaam Delhi Hong Kong Istanbul Karachi Kolkata
Kuala Lumpur Madrid Melbourne Mexico City Mumbai Nairobi
São Paulo Shanghai Taipei Tokyo Toronto

OXFORD is a trade mark of Oxford University Press in the UK and in certain other countries

National Library of Australia
Cataloguing-in-Publication data:

Allen, Matthew, 1965-.
Smart thinking: skills for critical understanding & writing.

2nd ed.
Bibliography.
ISBN 0 19 551733 4.

1. Critical thinking. 2. English language - Rhetoric. 3. Reasoning (Psychology). 4. Thought and thinking. I. Title.

153.42

Typeset by OUPANZS
Printed through Bookpac Production Services, Singapore

Contents

Preface to First Edition

The study and teaching of critical thinking (also known as informal logic) is relatively rare in Australia. There is little to guide the keen student or teacher in the development of skills for analysis and reasoning in everyday work and study. The orientation of most of the available books on this subject is more traditionally logical, and this orientation further complicates the process of teaching and learning applied critical thinking skills, since it tends to remove the use of reasoning and logical analysis from even its most basic social contexts.

Smart Thinking is designed to provide a simple, but not simplistic, guide for the development of critical thinking and analytical skills. It combines the undoubted strengths of the informal logical approach with a newer—but often-overlooked—insight: that reasoning and analysis are always communicative acts. I would not pretend that one can easily resolve the epistemological tensions between, on the one hand, the commonly held commitments to objective judgment and truth that underpin 'logic' as a mode of analysis and, on the other, the social relativism and intersubjectivity that a communicative-theory approach demands. However, from a pragmatic point of view, there is considerable profit to be gained from letting these two distinct approaches jostle alongside one another. Moreover, for all my attempts to keep competing epistemological ideas to a minimum in *Smart Thinking*, the book cannot remain purely 'practical'. Simple advice on 'better thinking' rubs up against deep and important matters of philosophy in a way that, I hope, creates a constructive interaction between the ease with which one can begin to improve one's thinking and the complexity of thinking *about* smart thinking.

While I myself work theoretically within post-structuralist frameworks, *Smart Thinking*'s bias towards communicative issues stems primarily from the very practical experiences I had in developing and teaching a critical thinking unit (Applied Reasoning 200) at Curtin University of Technology in Perth. On the basis of my experiences with many hundreds of students, I am confident in asserting that it is wrong to divorce analytical thinking from its communicative context. Outside the narrow confines of some academic disciplines, communication takes place on a vast scale, with far too little critical analysis to support it. It is precisely at the junction between 'knowledge as something one knows' and 'knowledge as a function of communication' that most of us need assistance in sharpening up our thinking skills.

My work in Applied Reasoning 200 has not only helped my own development as a critical thinker but has given me the opportunity to test ideas and approaches on a captive audience. So, my first debt of gratitude is to all the students who have, in so many ways, contributed to the writing of this book. Applied Reasoning 200 also became the focal point for a series of collegial relationships from which I have benefited enormously. For their assistance, insights (and perseverance with often impractical ideas), my thanks are extended to Patrick Bertola, Gina Koczberski, Des Thornton, and especially, Eamon Murphy, all of Curtin University. Thanks also to Will Christensen, Dennis Taylor, and Roy Jones for their positive encouragement as heads of academic departments. I also owe a debt of gratitude to Richard Bosworth, who some years ago, when I began to study at university, first taught me that critical enquiry involves asking about the 'who', 'when', 'why', and 'how', as well as the 'what' that was the staple of high school study. Michelle Forster and Emma Rooksby provided invaluable research assistance and general help; both are fine young philosophers. Thanks, as well, to my publisher, Jill Lane, and editor, Lucy Davison, of Oxford University Press. Finally, I could not have written this book without the unstinting support and reassurance of my wife Jane and step-daughter Verity; most of all, they remind me that a person cannot live on logic alone and confirm in my mind that life must be lived, not just with analytical reserve, but also with passion and commitment.

Matthew Allen
Perth
September 1996

Preface to Second Edition

I have been fortunate enough to find that I was right to assume that a practical book on critical thinking skills set in the context of communication would be both popular and necessary. I continue to be involved in teaching critical thinking in the unit Applied Reasoning, which is now a part of some courses of study through Open Learning Australia (REA11—visit http://www.ola.edu.au), and is being revived on campus at Curtin University. I have also realised that, in writing *Smart Thinking*, I myself learnt as much as I would hope for its readers and so, in the end, it was an easy decision to produce a new edition.

This second edition reflects the experiences of teaching with *Smart Thinking* over the years since it was first published. In revising it, I have found that much of what I had originally written remains valuable, and that students have learnt from it. But I have also made some significant changes, including greater assistance in the earlier chapters to help readers with the more complicated skills and concepts, as well as expanding later chapters on reasoning and on research. The final chapter is now a fully worked example of the skills that underpin the whole book, providing a model for readers of the power and value of the approach I am outlining. I would hope that readers will now find the sometimes-confusing journey towards greater ability in critical thinking and reasoning just that little bit easier, and with a clearer goal ahead.

In writing the second edition, I have been aided greatly by Jane Mummery and Robyn Mayes, both fine teachers of critical thinking, who have struggled with the problems of the first edition in teaching Applied Reasoning and have generously provided advice on how I might improve it. To them both, I owe a great deal. I also wish to thank Christine Richardson with whom I taught elements of critical thinking and who gave me the opportunity to develop further my ideas about reasoning and research. To my long-suffering publishers at Oxford University Press, especially my editors Lucy McLoughlin, Anne Mulvaney, and Chris Wyness, great thanks and apologies for all the delays. Perhaps they could ask the government about its neglect of higher education and the consequent doubling of workloads since I wrote the first edition. And to Jane and Verity, this book is still and always for you both.

Matthew Allen
m.allen@curtin.edu.au
Perth
February 2003

How to Use this Book

To get the most out of this book, you will need to read it carefully chapter by chapter. The book builds sequentially, so that many of the ideas and concepts introduced in earlier chapters underpin more complex discussion of related issues in subsequent chapters. Also, as you go, you should do the exercises in each chapter. Do not check the answers until you have completed all of a particular exercise and are satisfied with them. When you turn to the Answers, Discussion, and Further Advice, you will see that, in most cases, there is further discussion of the issues and concepts relevant to each exercise. As much as you can, don't be tempted to look at the next set of answers until you have completed the exercises for them. Often, you will be asked to do an exercise in order to provide you with the experience necessary to get the most out of the further advice offered in the answers. And, when you have done the exercises and checked the answers, I expect you will need to reread and revise the chapter again.

After you have read a chapter, done the exercises, and checked the answers, look at the Concept Check and Review Exercise at the end of the chapter. The concepts introduced in each chapter are listed. You should briefly write down what you know about them, then turn to the Glossary to check your answers. There are, by contrast, no answers provided for the review questions that you will find at the end of most chapters. If you have understood and integrated the material in each chapter, you should be able to answer these questions confidently. If you cannot, then it is probably a sign that you have missed something.

Finally, you should integrate what you learn about reasoning in this book with the work or study you are doing at the moment. For example, when doing the exercises and review questions, you will often be called upon to use information from your own life as examples or basic material with which to do an exercise. The whole point of this book is to give practical, applied advice. I can provide the advice; you must apply it.

This book aims to provide you with structured information, exercises, and reflections to guide your own learning. Your investment of time and effort in working through this structure will provide you with considerable returns in improving your smart thinking.

1

Smart Thinking

> There is an inner logic, and we're taught to stay far from it
> It is simple and elegant, but it's cruel and antithetic
> And there's no effort to reveal it ...

Bad Religion, 'Inner Logic'[1]

What is smart thinking?

There are many words associated with what is, loosely, termed 'thinking'. We are often told to 'think about the issues', to 'analyse in more depth', to 'use reasoning', or to 'be rational'. Sometimes (perhaps with reference to computers, or to the legendary *Star Trek* character Mr Spock) we are told to 'be logical'. Often students are told that they must think 'critically' if they are to succeed. When people write essays or reports, they are usually advised to make sure that they have a good 'argument' or that they 'explain in detail'. But do students (and lecturers) really know what these words and phrases mean? Can we actually identify the key skills and underlying techniques that allow us to think better?

The answer is yes. Smart thinking means knowing how to:

- work out and express your main ideas
- plan your communication of ideas so that they can be clearly understood
- check to see if you have covered all the important parts of your topic

- establish a framework or structure in which your basic facts and evidence make sense
- present ideas by linking them together to convince readers of your conclusion.

Moreover, we must also relate thinking to knowledge and information (what we think about), and the processes of communicating our ideas, either in written or oral form. Thinking is one aspect of an integrated process of finding, analysing, and communicating information. Your thinking begins even when you are deciding 'what' to read and write about.

'Smart thinking' can assist you in:

- working out where and how to look for the information you need
- understanding that information in relation to your own work
- deciding which information is relevant to your topic and which is not
- identifying when you need to find out more information to make sense of a problem.

Smart thinking can also improve your capacity to set your communication in context. It alerts you to the importance of:

- your audience and their expectations of what you are doing
- the requirements upon you to communicate in a certain way in a certain situation
- your own assumptions and biases, and the role of society in forming those biases, which will need to be considered and explored through your communication.

To think smart, you must use reasoning. Reasoning is the basis of much of our thinking. It is often described simply as the process of thinking through and communicating our reasons for holding certain views or conclusions. Reasoning is, however, better defined as a process of understanding and exploring the relationships between the many events, objects, and ideas in our world. None of these individual 'items' can be meaningful in and of itself. An item can *only* be understood in relation to other ones. Reasoning enables us to get beyond a world of innumerable separate events, objects, and ideas. Using reasoning, we see that all these separate items are interconnected, and what we know about any particular object depends on our knowledge of *other* objects. Sometimes the connections are obvious; other times, they are much harder to see. Reasoning involves finding and expressing these connections or relationships so that each individual event, object, or idea is explicable in terms of other events, objects, or ideas.

Exercise 1.1

Smart thinking demands that we do more than just 'think' vaguely about things. Before we look at reasoning, the key underlying process of thinking, let's consider some common 'informal' ideas about thinking. Look at the four actions listed below and, writing on a piece of paper, list some examples in your own life of when you have successfully done these actions and why you did them. The answers contain more discussion of each one.[2]

- Ask questions (of ourselves and others)
- Seek out information
- Make connections
- Interpret and evaluate

Reasoning

Reasoning represents one of the great advances that human beings have made in their ability to understand and make sense of the world. It has been described as a 'complex weave of abilities that help you get someone else's point, explain a complicated idea, generate reasons for your viewpoints, evaluate the reasons given by others, decide what information to accept or reject, see the pros as well as the cons and so forth'.[3] Yet it is also the case that reasoning does not come naturally but must be learnt and can be improved.

Let us begin with an easy example. Imagine you hold an apple in one hand and an orange in the other. Now, at first sight, these two objects appear to be completely different; each would seem to be understandable only in its own terms—that is, in a way unique to each apple and each orange. However, we are better able to understand them and to communicate what we think about them when we start to make connections. Here are some examples:

- An apple is not an orange.
- An apple and an orange are similar: both are pieces of fruit.
- This apple will be, roughly speaking, the same as all the other apples I have eaten.
- If I eat this orange and I like the taste, then I can assume that generally I will like the taste of other oranges.
- You should eat this fruit because you are hungry.

Obviously, this list makes only a few simple connections between the two *particular* pieces of fruit that we are considering; it also makes a few connections between the orange and the apple and other pieces of fruit *generally*; and the latter connections relate fruit to people.

If we did not make these connections, then every time we ate an orange, for example, it would be a new experience. We would not be able to rely on past experience or on our experiences with other things; nor would we be able to make any predictions about future experience. Such a world might be interesting (as each morning you drank your orange juice and had a whole new experience), but it would also be extremely confusing. Moreover, if you think about a more complex example (say, deciding to study for a university degree) you can see that, without the ability to make connections between things, you would not be able to make your decision in the way that all of us take for granted (by thinking, for example, 'A university degree will help me get a better job'). When we start to make connections, we are able to know things of which we have no direct experience (and which may not yet have happened). Of course, since we live in a society in which reasoning is accepted as the main method of processing information, we already use reasoning, but we usually do not think about it.

Often, we can feel reasonably certain about our knowledge because it is based on evidence of things that we *do* know about. For example:

> In the past, when driving down the freeway after work, I have found that there is usually a traffic jam. Because of the traffic jam, it always takes a long time to get home. So, today, because I need to get home quickly, I had better leave work earlier.

The conclusion that 'I had better leave work earlier' *follows from* the evidence or reasons given for it. We can say that it is a 'reasonable' conclusion. Using reasoning requires us to look for and rely on structures of connections between separate things or events in the world; it also requires us to make an active effort to create these structures—to make the connections that we cannot easily see.

The two main kinds of relationships that underpin these structures are:

- how things relate to one another, at any given moment (syntagmatic relationships such as 'an orange is a citrus fruit' or 'citrus fruits are edible')
- how things relate to one another, over time (paradigmatic relationships such as 'eating too many oranges made me feel sick' or 'if I want vitamin C, then I should eat an orange').

Working out the precise relationship requires attention to a number of 'patterns' that might help us to see how one thing is linked to another. These patterns can be understood through concepts such as:

- similarity/difference
- commonality/inconsistency
- necessity and sufficiency.

When we make these connections, we are able to function much more effectively and to make sense of the world around us. In particular, we are more capable of communicating our ideas and discussing knowledge with other people.

The things, then, that we do with reasoning, as a form of communication, are:

- **arguing** ('You should not believe what you see on television because ... ')[4]
- **explaining** ('Digital television has been introduced because ... ')
- **making decisions** ('I think we should buy a digital television receiver because ... ')
- **predicting the future** ('I expect digital television to make pay television better because ... ')
- **exploring issues** ('How will digital television link to the Internet?')

- **finding answers** ('Why did the government decide on a higher-quality digital television standard?')
- **justifying actions** ('When first introduced, I thought subscribing to pay television was not a good idea because ... ').

So, smart thinking is about reasoning, which is about the use and communication of knowledge. Researching, reading, analysing, testing, checking, planning, and writing all depend on understanding those interrelationships. Once you understand that knowledge consists of innumerable interrelations between small 'bits' of information, then you will be able to find, shape, and use knowledge for yourself.

But reasoning is also about people: the authors and audiences of arguments, explanations, and so on. And it is in relation to the human, social aspect of reasoning that we must really be 'smart'. Reasoning is *not* just formal logic; nor is it an abstract way of thinking about ideas. It is always a social act. People always use reasoning for particular purposes (be they economic, political, or whatever). They all have different perspectives on the issues being debated. Their age, class, race, gender, and ethnicity all influence the broad structures upon which they rely in reasoning. If we forget that reasoning has this social aspect, then we will run the risk of failing to think effectively (this point will be explored in more detail in later chapters). The connections and relations between ideas, events, proposals, and so on only become meaningful in the context of how, when, where, and why they are communicated with others.

How do we study smart thinking?

Thinking about thinking

Reasoning is something we already do: all of us have learnt, in one way or another, to think and to reason, to make connections and see relationships between various events and attitudes in our world. So, being a smart thinker is not about becoming a different sort of person, but about *improving* skills that you already have. The way to achieve this goal (and the main emphasis within this book) is to become explicitly aware of the analytical processes involved in reasoning. If you do, then you will be able to analyse complex issues more deeply, understand and process information more effectively, and communicate your ideas convincingly.

In succeeding chapters, then, we will learn a way of talking and thinking about reasoning that allows us to understand and use reasoning better. In particular, we will learn about the 'analytical structure' of ideas, which is, essentially, the clearest expression of reasoning. However, we usually encounter such structures 'embedded' in the words we read and hear, or in so-called 'natural language'. We must learn to distinguish more effectively between the structures and the natural language through which it comes to us. We will also encounter the idea of 'analytical questions', which can guide the way we think about and develop the relationships that comprise our analytical structures.

Thinkers with attitude

Remember, smart thinking always has a social dimension: we humans are doing the reasoning. As a result, one of the key ingredients of successful thinking and analysis, and of the effective use of reasoning, is our own attitude. For most (if not all) of us, our knowledge will usually consist of both the basic information or 'facts' we know, as well as a framework or structure of broader ideas with which we interpret these facts. Many of us are quite capable of assimilating and 'knowing' the facts, but smart thinkers constantly assess their structures and frameworks. In the process, they develop a much deeper and more effective appreciation of situations and events. Smart thinkers can be confident in their reasoning, precisely because they do not rely on too many unexamined or unquestioned assumptions.

First of all, we should always be willing to reflect on our own views and positions—to scrutinise the way we think about the world. We might ask ourselves, from time to time:

- Are my views consistent with one another?
- What assumptions underpin my views?
- Am I open to new ideas and alternative conclusions?
- Can I look at this issue from another perspective?

We should also be constantly asking ourselves, in relation to the issues that matter to us:

- Why did this happen?
- What should we do next?
- What does it mean?

As we will see, questioning is the key analytical skill that enables us to develop complex knowledge about the world in the form of structures of related ideas, so as to communicate with other people.

It is not the answers to these questions that matter, but the very fact that we ask them of ourselves, the willingness not to 'take things for granted' or to be satisfied with the 'obvious answer'. Indeed, a great failure of our society is that, by and large, we are people who believe that someone has the answer and all we have to do is develop a clever way of finding that answer. In fact, the key skill that you need, to be an effective and thoughtful adult who is able to engage with and understand the world, is *not* an ability to find the answers: it is the ability to *ask the right questions*. If you can ask the right questions, then most of the answers will come very easily. Moreover, you will also be able to determine why others do not necessarily accept *your* answers but have their own views. Questions are fundamental to reasoning.

Exercise 1.2

On a piece of paper, write down a key issue that you are dealing with at the moment—at work, perhaps an assignment, or something significant to you; don't choose a matter that is personal and emotional since these are often best analysed in different ways. Then start to ask yourself, in your mind, questions that will help to analyse that issue. As you go, write them down on the page, review them, and add more questions. Try to ask questions that are prompted by the first questions you thought of, questions that 'connect' the dots between the issue and another question.

Why do we need to 'think smart'?

Basically, unless we are smart thinkers, we cannot understand the world as well as we should; we cannot solve problems effectively and consistently; we cannot be successful in the areas of our life that concern information. Knowledge is the 'stuff' of everyday life in the early twenty-first century. We are always being asked to find it out, develop it, communicate it, and think about it. Smart thinking improves the ways in which we can work with knowledge and information.

First of all, smart thinking *helps you to study*. All academic work requires the use of reasoning. You want to understand the content, to digest information, pick out the key issues to learn, grasp the underlying concepts, and come to terms with unfamiliar ideas: reasoning is the way to go. Most teachers look for reasoned explanations and arguments when marking assignments. More importantly, by using smart-thinking skills to understand context—the situations in which we learn and communicate knowledge—you can understand the system you are in, the expectations and requirements on you as students, and then fulfil those requirements.

Second, smart thinking *helps you at work*. Work is, by and large, about decision making. It involves initiating change, coping with new and unfamiliar situations, finding better ways of doing things, finding out crucial information, understanding the people and institutions you work with, and solving complex problems. You use reasoning to accomplish these tasks, and if you have smartened up your thinking, then you will have more confidence in your abilities and succeed more often. In particular, the insights gained through smart thinking will assist in promoting more effective communication. Such communication is essential to successful business and professional life.

Third, and perhaps most importantly, smart thinking *makes you an active member of communities*. We are all members of various local and national groups and communities. While our membership of these communities gives us certain rights (for example, the rights of citizenship), it also entails certain responsibilities. It is our responsibility to understand what is happening in society and to act where necessary to conserve or change, to get involved, to make things better, and to fight injustice. We can only pick our way through the complex tangle of opinions, assertions, ideas, and assumptions that make up the dominant social world in which we live *if* we use the skills of smart thinking. Otherwise we are just going to be swept along without any control over events, a situation that is unhelpful for us as individuals but worse for the overall community, to which we owe the responsibilities that come with our rights.

Moreover, as the neo-punk band Bad Religion sing, there is an inner logic to the events that surround and involve us and, very often, we *are* taught to stay far from it. We often think that the best way to live our lives is to stay out of the way. As the song 'Inner Logic' continues: 'don't ask questions, don't promote demonstration/don't look for new consensus/don't stray from constitution'. There are two equally undesirable extremes in this refusal to think things through. At one extreme, staying away from the 'logic' means putting too much faith in so-called 'scientific', 'objective' knowledge (which appears as if it can never be questioned). At the other extreme, we shy away from complexity by putting too much reliance on individual relativism, in which each person's opinion is thought to be as good as anyone else's. We should never assume that there can be only *one* right view; we should not, in turn, presume that *all* views are right.

We *do* need to make the 'effort to reveal' the logic, to 'pierce the complexity', not only for ourselves but for the common good. Smart thinking is how to do it. Generally, knowledge is tied up in contexts of power and influence, and is hardly ever 'objective' or 'neutral'. Smart thinking can help empower us in the face of knowledge, revealing its political and social purposes, its biases and consequences, its exclusions and errors. Thinking smart is about recognising the contexts of power and influence in which knowledge exists. Thinking smart is about using knowledge within and against the constraints of these contexts. It also always involves remembering that our own reasoning may equally involve the exercise of power and of influence.[5]

Review exercise

There is no review exercise for this chapter—move on to chapter 2. Also, there is no need to do a concept check now. When you have finished the book, however, return to this chapter and revise it. I am sure you will read it with a very different perspective.

NOTES

1   From Bad Religion, *Stranger than Fiction* (compact disc), Dragnet, 1994, MATTCD003.
2   Developed from Josina M. Makau, *Reasoning and Communication: Thinking Critically about Arguments*, Wadsworth, Belmont, CA, 1990.
3   Stephen Toulmin, Richard Rieke, and Allan Janik, *An Introduction to Reasoning*, Macmillan, New York, 1984, p. 6.
4   An argument, here, does not mean a 'fight' or 'dispute' but is the technical name for reasoning that seeks to establish a conclusion on the basis of reasons.
5   These issues—objectivity, relativism, and so on—are complex. We will encounter them again in later chapters (chapters 6, 8, and 9). You should also be aware that there are legitimate differences of opinion on these matters among intellectuals.

2

Claims:
The Key Elements
of Reasoning

This chapter begins our in-depth exploration of how to use reasoning more effectively in order to make us smart thinkers. As suggested in chapter 1, learning to use reasoning better requires that we be more aware of what we are already doing. We need to learn some basic terms and concepts with which to talk and think *about* reasoning. The aim of this chapter is to improve our awareness of how we are actually *doing* reasoning. The focus in this chapter is on claims. In the next chapter we look at the process of linking claims together to form reasoning.

There are three main areas that we will cover in this chapter:

1   We will look at language, since reasoning is a way of manipulating and using words and statements. Language allows us to make claims about the world. Claims are the key component of reasoning.
2   We need to understand more about the significant properties of these claims which affect how we use them in reasoning.
3   We see how claims function differently, as premises or as conclusions, depending on how we link them together. The conclusion is what you are arguing for or explaining. The premises are how you get to your conclusion.

Understanding language

A basic look at language

Every time we argue or explain something, we use language—regardless of whether we are thinking to ourselves or communicating with others. As children, we learn to use language so 'naturally' that we tend to take its use for granted. In fact, there are many subtleties and complexities in language. Knowing something about these can help our reasoning by giving us more conscious control over the material (language) with which we are reasoning. There are four distinct 'levels' of language-use that build together to create 'language' as we know it.

The first level is a *word*—for example, 'student' or 'reasoning'—which is the basic unit of language. Words have meanings, usually more than one, and often multiple meanings are 'denotative' (that is, what the word explicitly says) or 'connotative' (the more subtle, 'hidden' meanings of words). We will see, through this book, that definitions of words are important but, for the moment, we are just interested in words insofar as they can form statements.

When we put some words together, we get the second level of language: a *statement*, such as 'there are several hundred students who have studied smart thinking at Curtin University'. We probably think of statements as being the same things as sentences, but they are not. In the following example we can see how one sentence can be made up of more than one statement: 'We use reasoning everyday of our lives, but most of us have no formal training, and the more practice and the more training, the better we will be at it'. The first statement is 'We use reasoning everyday of our lives'; the next is 'most of us have no formal training [in reasoning]'; the third is 'the more practice and the more training, the better we will be at it [reasoning]'.

The third level of language-use is the *text*, which is made up of any group of statements, such as the sentence above. Now, usually, the texts we encounter are much longer than just a few statements (for example, this book is a text, as is a newspaper article). But, remembering that we are talking about something different to 'natural' things we read and hear, we define a text as a group of statements that is of any length, so long as there is more than one statement and these statements are related to one another in some way. Texts are not just lists of statements; they are groups of connected statements. In the example of a multi-statement sentence from the previous paragraph, as well as in single statements, words like 'but' or 'and', and punctuation like commas and semi-colons, are not included in the statements. They act both to distinguish one statement from another and, at the same time, to join together the various statements to make a text. Practical communication via texts depends on the way these words connect the statements.

Finally, the last level of language-use is the *context*, which consists of all the elements outside a particular text that make it meaningful. Contexts cannot be 'seen' in the way, say, that the text you are now reading can be. A context for this book would include (at least) the purposes and goals of its author and readers, the assumptions about the meanings of words and ideas that lie behind it, and other texts that, though absent, are implicitly connected with what is being written and read here. For example, a student who reads this book as the textbook for the Open Learning Australia unit Applied Reasoning has a very different context to someone who is just browsing through it, casually looking for quick ideas about critical thinking.

Assumptions are a primary component of context. Assumptions are those ideas or values that we 'take for granted' and do not question. To be smart thinkers we must recognise the assumptions that surround us (including our own) and that influence every argument and explanation. Reasoning involves making connections between our ideas about the world, expressing them as linked claims, and constructing a text to express that knowledge. Obviously this reasoning is a conscious process, but it also draws upon a background of implicit or *assumed* connections and structures. As we grow up and learn about our environment (from parents, school, and so on), all sorts of connections are made for us and become embedded in our minds, so that we do not even realise we are relying on these structures when we think. For example:

> In the nineteenth century, Australian children were often warned that the 'black bogeyman' would get them if they were naughty. This apparently mild threat created an association in children's minds between 'Blacks' (indigenous Australians) and something dangerous. Is it any wonder, then, that when these children grew into adults they continued to act and think about indigenous Australians in extremely racist ways?

What makes assumptions dangerous is not their content (unlike the previous example, the content of assumptions may actually be correct) but, rather, that they are not consciously considered and tested to *see* if they are correct. What matters first is to be conscious of the assumption so we can ask 'is this true?'.

Smart thinkers must be capable of understanding how each of these four levels of language use relates to one another, and of how to write good statements, link them together to make a text, and consider the contextual factors that bear upon their text.

Statements that are claims

Our central focus for the moment is on a particular type of statement: the *claim*. Here are two examples of claims:

- Prior to the war on Iraq in 2003, more Australians opposed the war than supported it.
- John Howard, Australian Prime Minister in 2003, determined that Australian military forces should be deployed to participate in the war on Iraq.

Although these statements differ in what they say, each is a claim. More precisely, they claim to represent truly something 'real' about the world. We could test each claim to see if it is true or not (or at least get a clearer idea of whether or not we can accept it as true). For example, if someone claimed that John Howard had supported the war, we could check appropriate newspaper reporting of the time. Opinion polls conducted at the time can test the first claim, to see if there was such a majority. All statements that are claims assert the truth of some information or knowledge about the world.

Claims are *not*, as you might think, the opposite of facts. Nor does a claim 'become' a fact once we know it is true. A claim is always a claim, but the truth of some claims is established. And a claim does not necessarily involve some personal advantage or bias. Although in everyday speech we often use the word 'claim' to try to distinguish between statements whose truth is suspect or that are biased and those statements (called 'facts') whose truth is established and that are unbiased, these distinctions are dangerously misleading. All the statements that we think of as 'facts' are, actually, claims; they are so widely and clearly accepted as true that they *seem* different from claims that are not accepted. Put simply, claims are those statements that express beliefs or views about the way the world is or the way the world should be. Whether they are true or not is, of course, important, but it does not determine whether or not they are claims. The reasonableness of claims (what we think of as 'truth') does not change their status as claim or non-claim; but it does help us to decide what to do with claims in our reasoning (as we will see).

To emphasise this point, here are three statements that are *not claims*:

- Do you think Australia should continue to support all American foreign policy decisions concerning Iraq?
- Tell me immediately what you think about Australia's war on Iraq!
- G'day!

None of these statements expresses a view about the way the world is or should be, and hence they are not claims. The first asks for information (a *question*);[1] the second demands that a person do something (an *order*); and the third is an *exclamation*. Note how we do not say 'g'day' to claim that 'this day is a good day'. We say 'g'day' as a greeting, as a ritual use of language to begin a conversation. Similarly, orders and questions are ways of initiating or concluding communication. A few statements may fall somewhere between the two groups (claims and non-claims)—because they might be interpreted differently in different contexts—but generally speaking, all statements can be seen as one or the other.

We cannot tell just from the written or spoken expression of a statement whether or not it is a claim. Rather, we must look at the defining property of a claim: that it asserts something to be true.[2] To distinguish a claim from other sorts of statements, we simply need to consider whether it is *possible* to ask 'Is this statement true or false?'. A claim need not actually be true; it need not be false. It just has to be possible to ask if the claim *could* be true or false. Consider the following three statements. Which of them do you think are claims?

- Is the world round or flat?
- The world is round.
- The world is flat.

The first statement is not a claim—we cannot ask 'Is it true or false to say "Is the world round or flat"?'. But it is possible to ask 'Is it true or false to say "The world is round"?'. Similarly we can ask 'Is it true or false to say "The world is flat"?'. Hence the second and third statements are both claims, even though one is true and one is false. Claims are about the *possibility* of truth or falsehood, not about whether a claim really is true or not.

Exercise 2.1

Decide which of these statements are claims and which are not. Then write three examples of your own of statements that are claims and three examples of statements that are not.

a. Why did you do that?
b. There is a yellow marble on the table.
c. Get out of here!
d. Somewhere over the rainbow …
e. We should always pay our taxes on time.
f. Cheese is made from milk.

Claims as elements of reasoning

Effective thinking skills can be elusive. Reasoning has a structure and content that can be hard to control (as an author) and hard to discern (as a reader) when it is expressed in normal English (so-called 'natural language'). We tend to assume that claims are indistinguishable from their particular forms of expression, and it may be hard to grasp just what claims do within reasoning unless we shake them loose from their normal modes of expression. Claims may be expressed in natural language. However claims are better understood as *elements of reasoning*: the basic units of analysis in our arguments and explanations.

Written and spoken English does make claims, but draws them together and expresses them in ways that are stylish, but which also make it harder to identify and understand individual claims. In particular, sentences, which assist in making English easy to write and read, can obscure the more analytical function of the statements that these sentences express. Look, for example, at the following:

Many Australians favour making the nation a republic. However, it is unclear just how many Australians there are in favour of this, and until we know and are sure that a very large majority of Australians want a republic, we should not move too quickly to implement this change.

How do we identify the claims? In the first sentence, there is just one claim. In the second sentence, though, there are two claims. The first is 'it is unclear just how many Australians there are in favour of this' (note the use of 'this' to mean 'making the nation a republic'); the second is 'until we know and are sure that a very large majority of Australians want a republic, we should not move too quickly to implement this change'. Note how tricky the process of identifying claims can be. In the second sentence, the first 'and' indicates a break between two claims, but the word 'and' is later used differently to combine 'know and are sure'. Similarly, the comma after 'however' in the second sentence indicates that a claim is starting, but later on, a comma proves to be part of a claim. Note, too, the use of pronouns such as 'this' and 'it', which are used as substitutes for the actual nouns that claims contain.

As another example of this distinction between 'language for expression' and 'language for analysis', claims are sometimes expressed as questions. They appear as that special form of expression known as *rhetorical* questions, in which the answer to the question is presumed. For example, 'Isn't it obvious that Australia should be a republic?' is clearly different from 'Do you think that Australia should be a republic?'. The first question—a rhetorical question—is simply a clever way of saying 'Australia should be a republic', whereas the second question genuinely seeks an answer. Hence, to understand fully how claims are used in reasoning, we need to be aware of the difference between making claims as part of writing or talking, and making claims as part of the process of reasoning. Often, the claims we make in each context will be similar—but we cannot rely on it. Natural language, when properly put together in a narrative sequence, is an excellent tool for expressing our arguments and explanations. A danger, however, is that the requirement for proper, readable expression can confuse and mislead the unwary about the analytical units (claims) and structures (connections between claims) which, actually, constitute the reasoning.

Exercise 2.2

Identify the claims in the following sentences. Then write three sentences of your own, each of which expresses a number of claims in various different ways.

   a. All that glitters is gold, and this nugget glitters.
   b. Isn't it obvious that this song is called 'Diamonds are a Girl's Best Friend'?
   c. Silver jewellery is very common because silver is a cheap metal and it is easily worked.

More about claims
Connections within claims

A claim provides an *internal connection* between at least two ideas. For example, the claim that 'Australia should become a republic' provides an internal connection between, roughly speaking, 'Australia' and 'republic'. Similarly, 'Australia should not become a republic' also makes this connection, although the meaning of that claim is completely different. The technical, grammatical names for the two components within a claim are the 'subject' and the 'predicate' of the statement. Roughly speaking, the subject is the main focus of the claim, and the predicate is some property or consequence of, or notable point about, that subject and the way the claim is made is to identify through the verb the link between the subject and the predicate. Hence 'Reasoning is a skill' uses the verb 'is' to assert that reasoning is a member of the larger set of things we know about called 'skills'. As another example, 'Reading this book on critical thinking is no use if you are not practising critical thinking exercises' is also a claim with a more complicated link between the subject 'Reading this book on critical thinking', and a predicate 'not practising critical thinking'.

Exercise 2.3

Identify the subject and the predicate in the following statements:

  a. Drinking milk makes some people feel sick.
  b. I do not drink milk.
  c. Milk drinking is not recommended for people who are lactose-intolerant.

This property of a claim—an internal connection between two or more ideas— is fundamental. The internal connection underpins the external links between claims that are necessary in reasoning. While reasoning does not consist simply of one claim, it does occur when you take a number of claims and, by varying the pattern of interconnections, produce a 'link' from the first interconnection to the next. Here is a simple example (we will be doing much more on this concept in later chapters).

> Reasoning is a skill. Skills can be improved by practice. The book *Smart Thinking* gives you a chance to practise reasoning. Reading *Smart Thinking* and doing the exercises will improve your reasoning.

See how the same ideas get used, but in a different order? These claims, because they share the same ideas even though in some the idea is the subject and in others it is the predicate, are well on the way to being used for reasoning. So, to reason, we always need more than one claim, all linked together in some way. It is this internal connection within a single claim that allows these external links to be made.

Claims that include claims

One example of the importance of grasping this process of internal connection is provided by a special kind of claim in which an entire claim serves as one element of another claim. We find two main uses of this kind of claim-formation. First, there are claims such as 'George W. Bush said that Saddam Hussein was an evil dictator'. In this claim, what is being asserted is that George W. Bush has said those words, and not that Hussein was such a person. The claim 'Saddam Hussein was an evil dictator' here serves as the predicate to the subject 'George W. Bush', connected with the word 'said'. Thus, if we were to assess the truth of the claim, it would do no good to see whether or not Hussein was a dictator or evil (even though we probably could find much evidence to support that point), because the claim is about what Bush said. These claims, which are essentially concerned with what others have already claimed, are vital: we often wish to reason about another's point of view and thus must understand how to make claims about that person and their words.

A second and even more important use for claims within claims can be found in claims that use propositional logic, that is, claims taking the 'if..., then...' form so common in contemporary philosophy and computer programming. Such a claim is, for example, 'If I am unwell, then I should go to the doctor'. Now it might look as though there are two claims here: and, indeed, there are. However, by placing two claims in an if/then relationship, each claim becomes a subsidiary part of a single, much more powerful claim. What is actually being asserted in the if/then claim is not the substance of one or the other claim but, rather, the relationship between them. Hence 'If I am unwell, then I should go to the doctor' asserts that it is reasonable to do something (go to the doctor) when a particular state of affairs (feeling unwell) occurs. We will see the importance of these special 'if/then' claims in chapter 3.

Exercise 2.4

Identify the claims within a claim here, remembering that an entire claim can serve as either predicate or subject.

a. I have been told by my doctor that drinking milk makes some people feel sick.
b. If I drink milk, then I feel sick.
c. If a person comes to a doctor and says 'If I drink milk, then I feel sick', then the doctor will diagnose that person as lactose-intolerant.

Scope and certainty

A statement that makes a claim about the world allows us to judge the truth or falsity of that statement. In making this judgment, we need to consider the *scope* of the claim. For example, each of these claims has a different scope:

- *All* Australians think global terrorism threatens this country.
- *Some* Australians think global terrorism threatens this country.
- A *few* Australians think global terrorism threatens this country.

The claims are very similar, except in their reporting of the number of Australians who believe global terrorism threatens their country. The scope, in each case, is determined by the different value of 'all', 'some', and 'few'. Scope is not just about numbers. It can also be seen in claims about, for example, a geographic area ('Most of Western Australia is uninhabited') or time ('For much of its history, Australia was not populated by white people').

Certainty is another characteristic of all claims. Whether explicitly stated or not, claims include a judgment about the likelihood or probability that what they are claiming is true, or will become true:

- There is a *high probability* that Australia will suffer a major terrorist attack in the next decade.
- There is *some chance* that Australia will suffer a major terrorist attack in the next decade.
- There is *virtually no chance* that Australia will suffer a major terrorist attack in the next decade.

In each case, the claims are saying something about Australia and terrorism; they differ only in their explicit statement of the probability that the substance of the claim will come true. Understanding how to include proper indications of scope and certainty in the claims you write, or to recognise them in other people's work, is crucial to being an effective reasoner. Remember, scope and certainty are tied in with the idea that claims are asserting the truth of something. If you limit or qualify your claims by appropriately indicating scope and certainty, then you are thinking more clearly and therefore can write better claims.

Exercise 2.5

Identify the two components that are internally linked within each of the following claims. Then rank claims a–c in order of scope (from widest to narrowest) and claims d–f in order of certainty (from most certain to least certain). In each case identify the word or words that lead you to your judgment. Then write a list of some of the other words that can be used to indicate the scope and certainty of a claim.

   a. Sometimes, when I drink milk, I feel sick.
   b. Whenever I eat cheese before sleeping, I have dreams.
   c. Occasionally, after eating rich food, I get indigestion.
   d. It is probable that humans will live in space.
   e. There is no way that humans can live in outer space.
   f. I'd say the odds are 50:50 that humans will live in space.

Descriptive and value claims

Some claims assert that things are, or have been, a certain way; and some claims make judgments about the way things should or should not be. These are respectively called descriptive claims and value claims. For example, 'This book is printed on white paper' describes the type of paper, whereas 'We should use less paper to save trees' expresses a value judgment ('it is good to save trees'). But, to complicate matters many, and perhaps even all, claims have some implicit value judgment. Often we find an implicit value judgment in the words that make up the claim. For example, 'This book is comprehensive' implies some positive value judgment, whereas 'This book provides only an outline of reasoning techniques' implies a more negative value judgment. So, really, there are two main sorts of value claims: those that explicitly declare a value judgment, and those whose value judgment is hidden in the choice of words.

There are also some claims that can legitimately be called descriptive claims. Yet, even then, claims are almost always found in combination with other claims. So, if there is one value claim among a series of claims, then all of them tend to create an implied value judgment. Here we can see that the context in which we find a claim—the purposes and processes by which a text, containing many linked claims, is produced and received—plays a very significant role. Claims that appear to their author as descriptive may, in the context provided by their readers, suddenly acquire value judgments. Hence, judgments of value can rarely be made solely on the basis of one claim; they depend on the other claims with which the claim is linked (the text) and the circumstances in which that text is presented (the context). Being alert to the value judgments that you read and make is a skilled smart thinking attribute.

Exercise 2.6

Decide which of these four claims are explicit value claims and which are implicit value claims that appear to be descriptive claims. You may also decide that some of the claims are purely descriptive and contain no value judgments. Then write three claims of your own, one of which is explicitly a value claim, one of which has a clear implied value judgment, and one of which is, in your opinion, clearly descriptive.

    a. Fatty foods are bad for you.
    b. Regular cows' milk contains fat.
    c. You should drink milk each day.
    d. Regular cows' milk is a white liquid.

Claims and reasoning
Using claims as conclusions and premises

We know that reasoning is, put simply, giving reasons for one's views. We reason, therefore, by linking claims together to form a text in which most of the linked claims provide a reason or reasons for accepting another claim, or the linked claims explain why another claim can be made. For example, if I said 'Australia should become a republic', it would only be natural for you to ask 'why?', which would prompt me to give you a reason: that 'Australia's economic relationship with Asia would be strengthened if Australia declared its final independence from its European origins by becoming a republic'.

The claims that act as reasons are 'premises' and the claim that is being supported or explained is the 'conclusion'. When reasoning, we will always be dealing with at least two claims: the claim we want people to accept and the claim we are using to support the first claim. Almost always there are a number of premises supporting one conclusion, but the minimum requirement is one premise and one conclusion. A fundamental skill in reasoning is to be able to identify, in our own and in others' work, those claims that are serving as premises to support the claim that is acting as a conclusion. Thus we need to understand how claims can be used as conclusions and premises.

To do so, we must remember that, before we use them in reasoning, all premises and conclusions are the same thing: they are claims. There is nothing about a claim on its own that makes it a conclusion or a premise. Until we decide, in our reasoning, that claim Z will be the conclusion and claims X and Y will be the premises, X, Y, and Z are all just claims. They only become premises and conclusion through the act of linking them together, as in 'Because of X and Y, my conclusion is Z'. The difference between premises and conclusions is not dependent on any essential qualities of the claims; it is, instead, a *functional* difference. Whether a claim is a conclusion or a premise depends on the function that the claim performs in any particular argument or explanation. What determines that function is the *relationship* between one claim and another.

Let us use the following claims to demonstrate this point:

- Your car is dirty.
- You drove the car through some mud.
- You should wash your car.

And here are two very simple examples of the way we can use these claims in reasoning, with the claims marked as [c] (conclusion) or [p] (premise) to show how they perform different functions:

- Your car is dirty [c] because you drove through some mud [p].
- You should wash your car [c] since your car is dirty [p].

The same claim—'Your car is dirty'—is used in two different ways: first, as a conclusion being explained and, second, as a premise. The general rule, thus demonstrated, is that any claim can be either a conclusion or a premise depending on how it is linked with other claims and the context in which it is used.

Conclusions and premises are very similar because both are claims. However, within reasoning, some claims serve a different purpose to other claims. The nature of premises and conclusions is not already laid down, magically, in the words we use to express them, but is something that we can actively control and alter. For example, we may read someone else's conclusion and then use it as a premise in our own reasoning. Or, we see that the premises of someone's argument need further explanation and, by using them as conclusions, proceed to give that explanation with our own premises.[3]

Exercise 2.7

Make up four short examples of reasoning using the following claims. Make sure that you practise using the same claim as the conclusion in one example and as a premise in another.

- The road is wet.
- You need to drive more carefully.
- You should pay attention to what you are doing.
- Verity has just come home soaking wet.
- There was a rainstorm a few minutes ago.

More on conclusions

So, when we reason, we first of all have to decide which is the claim we are trying to argue for or explain. This claim is the conclusion. It is not a summary, but a new statement altogether, which may be linked to the premises but goes beyond them to give some further information, the 'truth' of which becomes clearer because of the premises given. The conclusion is a claim in its own right, and not merely a restatement of the claims already made as premises.

The selection of a conclusion is dependent on the *purpose* of our overall argument or explanation. First, we can use claims about the future as conclusions. These sorts of conclusions are required when we are making a *prediction*, as in 'In the future, the world will be much warmer [c] because of the effects of industrial pollution [p]'. Predictions are always doubtful since the events they predict have not yet happened, and thus their truth can never be established except as a prediction. Hence they require supporting argument to make them acceptable. We can also use claims about the past or the present to *establish* what is the case. Often there are doubts about what has happened or is happening (for example, in a criminal investigation), and argument can be used to support our conclusions on these matters.

Second, we can use as a conclusion any claim that makes an appeal for people (whether an individual or group) to act in a certain manner, as in the argument that 'We should reduce the production of carbon monoxide [c] because this action will reduce the rate of global warming [p]'. Such arguments, the conclusions of which are *appeals to action*, are designed to convince people to do something. Sometimes the action required is for us to think differently, as in an argument that demands that 'You should not think highly of governments that are reluctant to stop global warming [c] since these governments are risking the future prosperity of all humanity [p]'.[4]

Conclusions such as those just discussed require arguments to convince audiences to accept them. In both cases, it is the conclusion that is in doubt (remember that claims are statements that may or may not be true). But other conclusions, often about events happening in the past, are not in doubt, but still involve reasoning that *explains* why the conclusion can be made. In the sentence 'We now have a problem with global warming [c] because previous governments were blind to the consequences of industrial growth and technology [p]', the conclusion reports that there is now a problem with global warming so that the premise can explain why this has happened. Some explanations can be characterised as *justifications*, as in 'I decided to vote for the Greens at the last federal election [c] because I am very keen to see Australia's environment protected [p]'. In this example, the conclusion reports something that happened so that the writer can justify why they did it.

Exercise 2.8

Try to work out what sort of conclusion is used in each of the following. Remember to think about the purpose that the conclusion is designed to fulfil. In each example the conclusion is the second claim in the sentence.

   a. Since the bushfire threat is high in the next three months, we should improve our fire-fighting service.
   b. Since there has been no rain recently, I forecast that there will be a high bushfire threat this coming summer.
   c. Because the government failed to improve the fire services, the bushfires that occurred in 2001 were much harder to control than in previous years.
   d. The government has not done much to improve the fire-fighting service—don't you think that it is inefficient?
   e. Because the budget deficit has required the government to make many cut-backs in spending, we have done little to increase available fire-fighting resources [assume that a government representative is speaking].

More on premises

While a basic outline of the different types of conclusions is relatively straightforward, there is no similar, straightforward approach for different types of premises. Virtually any claim you can think of can serve as a premise. Even claims that we might normally think of as conclusions can be premises. All that premises have to do is to be able to provide support for the conclusion (either in explaining it or arguing for it). Thus, premises tend in most cases to be initially more acceptable than the conclusion (though not always—see 'Strength of support' in chapter 6). Furthermore, it is misleading to think about individual premise 'types'; instead, we should look at the way in which premises connect with one another. In short, premises function in three ways: they make a substantive point (i.e. report something, or provide some kind of evidence), they can define some term in the argument, or they can frame the other premises, demonstrating more clearly the relationship of all the other premises to the conclusion (see chapter 4 for more details on how premises function).

Review

Words combine to form statements, which in turn combine to form texts. No text can be understood outside its context of use and interpretation. The most important statements for us to consider are claims. When properly linked together, they form a text, which is either an argument or an explanation. Claims state, in language, the events, ideas, and things that make up our world, asserting that what they represent is true. Claims are the key elements from which we build our arguments and explanations. The analytical function of claims is, however, often obscured by their mode of expression.

By understanding what claims are and what their properties are, we can better understand how to use claims as premises and conclusions in our reasoning. Claims have three significant properties. First, a claim always contains an internal connection between two or more components. One or both of these components can be a claim in its own right, but functioning differently—as an element within a claim. Second, claims always include some indication of scope and certainty, though often they are implied. Third, claims are either descriptive (what is) or are value judgments (what *ought to be*). Many claims appear to be descriptive but either contain implicit value judgments or become value-laden when read in combination with other claims.

Claims are used as either premises or conclusions; the difference between them is determined by how we use them in any particular act of reasoning. Any claim can serve as a premise or conclusion. That said, we can see how conclusion-claims must relate to the particular purposes of the reasoning: predicting, establishing, or appealing for action, and explaining or justifying. In the last case, the reasoning involves an explanation, whereas the other purposes require an argument.

CONCEPT CHECK

The following terms and concepts are introduced in this chapter. Before checking in the Glossary, write a short definition of each term:

argument

assumption

audience

certainty

claim

conclusion

connotation

context

descriptive claim

exclamation

explanation

internal connection

order

premise

purposes of reasoning

question

scope

statement

subject

text

value claim

word

Review exercise 2

Answer briefly the following questions, giving, where possible, an example in your answer that is different from those used in this book.

    a. Is a statement the same as a sentence? Why should we distinguish between the two?

    b. What distinguishes claims from statements that are not claims?

    c. Why are some claims thought of as 'facts'?

    d. What are the three crucial properties of claims?

    e. What is special about if/then claims?

    f. What is the difference between a premise and a conclusion?

    g. Are all conclusions the same? If not, why not?

    h. What determines the 'type' of a particular premise?

    i. What happens to claims when we express them in natural language?

NOTES

1   As we will see in chapter 8, questions can also be thought of as 'potential' claims or 'claims in question'. Here, for example, the claim 'Australia should continue to support all American foreign policy decisions concerning Iraq' has been put under scrutiny by turning it into a question.

2   There is considerable philosophical argument concerning the notion of truth. Some philosophers might wish to substitute words such as 'valid' or 'sound' in this test of a claim, but for the practical purposes of this book, 'truth' will suffice. In particular, however, we should recognise that value claims (described a little later in this chapter) cannot really be true or false, but they can be judged in terms of whether or not they are reasonable.

3   We cannot simply interchange conclusions and premises as we like and still be confident of being correct. It would, for example, be incorrect to say that 'because you should wash your car, your car is dirty'. We need to think much more carefully about the relationships we are asserting to be true when we decide just what exactly our premises and conclusions are. For example, the following would be good reasoning: 'I know that if you are told to wash your car, then it is more than likely that the car is dirty; I have just heard someone tell you to wash your car; therefore I can infer that your car is dirty (otherwise that person would not have told you to wash it)'. We should note here, too, that giving premises to explain a known conclusion is contextually different from giving premises to establish by argument the soundness of an unknown or doubtful conclusion. The term 'conclusion' here merely indicates the logical function of the claim we are explaining, and not its importance or significance. In an explanation, and from the point of view of our audience, our premises and how they explain the conclusion are more important than the conclusion itself.

4   Because group and individual decisions carry with them the requirement that we be able to justify and explain our decisions to others, decision making also involves reasoning.

3

Linking:
The Key Process
in Reasoning

Claims are the basic material of reasoning, but they must be linked together if we are to argue and explain our points of view. We have already seen that claims that are linked to a conclusion by supporting it or explaining it are called premises. A conclusion, therefore, is a claim that is supported or explained. In this chapter we investigate this linking process in more detail. My principal goal, again, is to give you greater awareness of how you reason, in order to improve what you actually do.

There are four main areas we will cover in this chapter:

1   We will examine natural language for the *traces* of this linking. Traces are the signals in natural language that we only half-consciously use to develop our reasoning within a narrative-flow format (what you normally read and write).

2   We will look at the process of linking *analytically*, introducing the idea that all important relationships between claims can be shown in a diagram. Combining the diagram with a list of claims provides a clear, analytical structure format without the confusions of natural language.

3   To assist in understanding the analytical structure format, we will learn about *casting* the reasoning of others, as a useful exercise for skill development.

4   We consider in more detail what we need to know in order to be comfortable expressing our critical thoughts in such a format, including the way in which complex argument forms can be shown using a diagram.

Links between claims

Evidence of the linking process

We can directly 'see' claims in natural language, but *linking*, the process of reasoning, can only be inferred, indirectly.[1] In any argument or explanation in natural language we can find the evidence of this linking process in the words or phrases that show or signal how one claim relates to another. We have already come across these words. Remember these examples?

- Your car is dirty [c] because you drove through some mud [p].
- You should wash your car [c] since your car is dirty [p].

The words 'because' and 'since' do *not* form part of the claims (the premises and conclusions) but link them together, signalling which claim is the premise and which the conclusion. These signal words are the visible traces of the *mental* process of linking.

Because of the richness and complexity of the English language, we rarely find evidence for every act of linking. Sometimes no link words are used because the sense of the reasoning is clear just from the arrangement of the claims; sometimes punctuation does the job. At other times, when it is stylistically appropriate, phrases or even sentences signal the linking process. Link words are not necessarily written directly between the premises and the conclusion, but since their function is not determined by their position in a text, they can nevertheless still signal which claim is which. In all cases, the linkages are between two or more claims, so that any link words can signal that both a premise and a conclusion are present and can distinguish between them.

Here are some examples:

- I found out today that I had passed my exam. I was elated. [The order of the sentences signals that the first claim is linked to the second claim as premise to conclusion.]
- Because I felt ill, I went home from work. ['Because' signals that 'I felt ill' is the reason that explains the conclusion 'I went home from work'; the comma serves to show that there are two claims here and, hence, that some link can be inferred.]
- We need to learn to think: it helps us to do better at work and to do better at university. [The colon separates the claims and, at the same time, links them. The sense of the sentence signals the link between the first part (the conclusion) and the second part (the premises).]
- John has passed his final exams. This means that he is a fully qualified lawyer. [The phrase 'this means that' is the linking element here: 'this' refers to the first claim and 'means that' signals that the second sentence contains a conclusion. Because the second claim is identified as a conclusion and is linked to the first, we know that 'John has passed his final exams' is a premise.]

- Everyone knows that Australia has great natural beauty and a marvellous climate, and that makes it clear why many tourists come here. ['Everyone knows that' signals that a premise or premises are following it, and 'that makes it clear why' links these premises to 'many tourists come here'—the conclusion that these premises explain.]

Exercise 3.1

Here are the five examples from above. Rewrite each of them so that the reasoning is the same (i.e. the same premise and same conclusion) but in a different way, thus helping you to see how natural language can vary widely and that there is an underlying logic which can be expressed in various ways.

    a. I found out today that I had passed my exam. I was elated.
    b. Because I felt ill, I went home from work.
    c. We need to learn to think: it helps us to do better at work and to do better at university.
    d. John has passed his final exams. This means that he is a fully qualified lawyer.
    e. Everyone knows that Australia has great natural beauty and a marvellous climate, and that makes it clear why many tourists come here.

Exercise 3.2

Here are three claims. Using the last claim as your conclusion and the first two as premises, write three different arguments in natural language and using a variety of different linking formations. Monitor the way in which the words reflect and signal your mental processes of linking premises and conclusions.

- The road is wet.
- Wet roads increase the risk of accident.
- You should drive more carefully.

The problem of understanding linkages

There are many different words and phrases that appear in natural language to link claims together explicitly. There are also many ways of writing claims so they are clearly linked. But the linkages are not dependent on having the link words there in your writing. If you think, for example, that 'Australia should become a republic because this change will make Australia a more independent nation', then the linkage of this conclusion with this premise occurs because you *think* it is so (so long as you have sound reasons for that thought). Link words such as 'because' are very useful as signposts, which you can use to help others follow your reasoning, but they are the result of your thought processes. Simply putting in a word such as 'thus' or 'because' cannot make unlinked claims magically become an argument.

In other words, we must think through the analytical structure of our ideas *before* we express them in words. If we do this, and have some proficiency in writing, then the proper signals and traces of our analysis will emerge through our texts. If we simply learn to 'write' (rather than 'think'), then it is unlikely that our analysis will improve. No matter how hard we try to 'write better', we will often fail.[2]

The complex ways in which we signal the links in language are well suited to the requirements of naturally *expressing* our arguments and explanations. But they impede us in trying to understand and control our reasoning processes. First of all, links between claims precede and exist independently of their written expression. Because of the ways in which we use language, it is often hard to see the 'logic' in what someone is saying or writing, and probably harder still to write and speak ourselves in ways that make clear to our audience just what the reasoning is behind our views. The solution is to find a format or way of writing that breaks reasoning down into two components: first, the claims and, second, the way in which they are linked together.

The analytical structure of reasoning

Representing the analytical structure

There two ways of understanding what we read and write. First, there is what I am calling the *narrative flow*, that is, words arranged into sentences, and then divided into paragraphs. Second, there is the analytical structure, which is expressed in a list of claims and a diagram or picture showing how they are related to one another. Imagine that we have been asked to give our views on the environment by stating one action that people should take to help improve the world's environment. The following is an argument on this topic in the narrative flow format:

> All motor cars should be fitted with devices that reduce the pollution caused by their exhausts. My reasoning for this view is as follows. Car exhaust emissions are one of the most significant causes of air pollution, and if we are going to tackle the problem of improving the environment, we should concentrate on the major causes of pollution. Also, it is relatively simple to fit the appropriate anti-pollution device and will not cause dramatic social and economic upheavals in the way people live.

But there is another way to express the argument, picking out the key claims and the links between them:

1. All motor cars should be fitted with devices that reduce the pollution caused by their exhausts.

2. Car exhaust emissions are one of the most significant causes of air pollution.
3. If we are going to tackle the problem of improving the environment, we should concentrate on the major causes of pollution.
4. It is relatively simple to fit the appropriate anti-pollution device.
5. Fitting appropriate anti-pollution devices will not cause dramatic social and economic upheavals in the way people live.

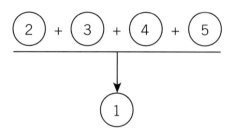

Can you see how the two forms (narrative flow and analytic structure) say roughly the same thing? In the narrative flow, the linking phrase 'My reasoning for this view is as follows' signals that the following claims are premises for the conclusion before them. In the diagram, this connection is indicated by the arrow symbol [↓] connecting claims 2–5 with claim 1. In such a diagram we always put the conclusion-claim at the bottom (no matter what number we give it). We do this because, logically, the premises *lead to* the conclusion, and positioning the conclusion at the bottom reminds us of this crucial process. So, obviously, the premises go *above* the conclusion.

Certain words in the narrative flow, such as 'and' and 'also', are not included in the numbered list of claims. Why? Well, because the work that those words do (tying the premises together) is shown in the analytical structure diagram by the plus symbol (+). Furthermore, to indicate that all four premises work together to support the conclusion, the diagram uses a horizontal line to 'group' these premises (___). Finally, note that claims explicitly state the missing subject which was not included in the narrative flow.

What the analytical structure format offers

The analytical structure format, then, is a much clearer way of showing the exact claims being made and the ways in which they relate to one another. This format, by representing the connections between claims through the standardised form of the diagram, avoids all of the vagaries of the English language that we have already seen, with its myriad ways of signalling what is the conclusion and what are the premises. By listing the claims as distinct entities, it also overcomes complex sentence formations, with multiple claims within sentences, claims within claims, half-expressed claims, and so on. All the potentially confusing 'short-hand' use of pronouns, such as 'this' and 'it', and implicit cross-referencing is removed in favour of precisely written claims. Finally, the diagram, with grouped premises, clarifies all of the clever ways of writing that make English interesting to read but that mean it is hard to recognise just exactly which premise leads to which conclusion, and in combination with which other premises.

Here is a more complex example of how one argument can be expressed in two different formats—as narrative flow and as analytical structure. While there is much about this argument that you may not yet understand (and we explore the details in later chapters), for the moment, just use it as a point of comparison between the two formats. First, here is the underlying structure, expressed as a list of claims and a diagram to show how they relate to one another.

1. The Internet has no single regulatory body to impose censorship.
2. The Internet is hard to censor consistently and reliably.
3. The Internet is a new communications medium that is available for anyone to use.
4. Vast amounts of violent and pornographic material are available on the Internet.
5. Children often have access to the Internet.
6. Children will, sooner or later, view violent and pornographic material on the Internet.

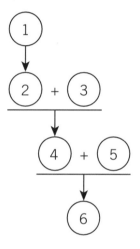

And here is how we might write this argument in natural language.

We need to be keenly aware that children will, sooner or later, view violent and pornographic material on the Internet. It is a new communications medium that is available for anyone to use. The 'Net', since it has no single regulatory body to impose censorship, cannot be consistently and reliably censored, meaning that vast amounts of violent and pornographic material are available on it, and as we know, children often have access to the Internet.

Exercise 3.3

Using the above example about the Internet, briefly list the differences and similarities between the two formats. *Check the answers carefully.*

For simple examples, such as the first one I gave, it may seem foolish to use another format when the narrative flow (with which we are all more familiar) seems to work well enough. Equally it may seem that, in longer examples, such as the second one, the analytical structure only complicates the business. These observations miss the point: we need to be able to see the content and structure of reasoning (claims and a diagram) clearly before we can learn about, and thus smarten up, our thinking.

Learning more about the analytical structure
The analytical structure behind narrative flow

The primary purpose of the analytical structure format is to assist you in planning your own writing. However it is very useful to look at other people's reasoning as a way of learning about it. We can recover this analytical structure by, first, finding the claims being made and, second, grasping the connections between them (some signals of which can be found in the traces of reasoning represented by any linking words or phrases). Before moving on to look at how we can use the analytical structure in our own writing, let us use it as a tool to understanding other people's reasoning.

Casting

The process by which we recover an analytical structure from a written argument is called 'casting'.[3] I will work through an example, step by step, and then provide some practice examples. We will use the following natural argument—a very simple one that I have constructed to help demonstrate this process.

> Let's consider the facts. Chemical factories are very dangerous to live nearby and one has been built near your house. You'd be crazy to put yourself in danger, no? That's why you should move and live somewhere else.

Before beginning, make sure you understand what you are reading and remember that you are not doing the reasoning here and must try to stay true to what is written, even if you disagree with it.

So, what is the *first* step? Earlier in this chapter, we looked at how natural language contains 'traces' of reasoning—words that are not part of the claims, but which represent the way the author is linking those claims together. I will underline the words that signal reasoning:

> <u>Let's consider the facts</u>. Chemical factories are very dangerous to live nearby and one has been built near your house. You'd be crazy to put yourself in danger, no? <u>That's why</u> you should move and live somewhere else.

The *second* step is the crucial one: identify and mark the claims that are being made. We have already looked at the properties of claims in chapter 2 and here you see why that discussion is so important. The easiest way to mark these claims is by putting them in parentheses. I have also numbered the claims because we need to diagram their interrelationship later.

> Let's consider the facts. (Chemical factories are very dangerous to live nearby) 1 and (one has been built near your house) 2. (You'd be crazy to put yourself in danger) 3, no? That's why (you should move and live somewhere else) 4.

Finally, we need to draw a diagram that shows how these claims link together. The conclusion always comes last and the premises go above it.

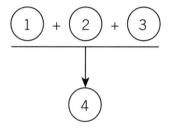

How did I work out what the conclusion was? Look at the linking phrase 'That's why' in the last line. 'That' refers to all the things previously said and 'why' here means 'these are the reasons that explain or justify why something else is reasonable'. So, on that basis, I have determined that the author intended the last claim as the conclusion, with the other claims being the premises that form one reason why that conclusion is justified.

Also, note that I have had to deal with a contracted claim: 'one has been built near your house'. If we were writing this claim out formally, it would be 'A chemical factory has been built near the house where you live' but, in natural language, the narrative flow means the author instead has written 'one', referring back to 'a chemical factory' in the first claim and 'your house', implying a connection to 'live' in the first claim. A key part of good casting (and indeed good reading) is to be able to see the contractions necessary for good narrative flow and yet recognise the substance of the analytical claims being made.

Exercise 3.4

Now you practise it. Here are four short arguments or explanations, each with a different structure, and each with a little 'trick' to watch out for. Try underlining the signals of linking, delineating the claims, and, using a diagram, show how they relate to one another. Check the answers carefully for more advice on casting.

Remember, what matters most here is correctly identifying the claims—and claims may not be written out as 'neatly' as you would like.

a. I should not buy a car at the moment. I have just lost my driver's licence, and besides, I can't afford it.

b. Nicole Kidman is an international movie star, and I know that, as a general rule, international movie stars get paid a lot of money. Therefore, it is obvious that Nicole Kidman is well paid.

c. I have not got a university education, whereas several of my colleagues do. All of them have recently received promotions, but I did not receive one. Given that we are all roughly equal in our job performance, I would have to conclude that a university education really helps one to get ahead in a career.

d. What was the explanation for Sydney beating Beijing for the 2000 Olympics? There were two main reasons. The Sydney organisers did a better job of lobbying the International Olympic Committee delegates and, because of political crises in China at the time and perceived doubts about Beijing's quality of services and venues, Sydney offered a much safer venue for a successful Olympic games.

If you have checked the answers to these four problems, you will realise that there is a lot more to learn about exactly how reasoning works in linking claims together. It is not simply a matter of working out which claims are the premises and which are the conclusions. You should also realise that casting is not an exact science—it is a tool to help you unpick the reasoning of others and, for our purposes, is mainly designed to help you get better at your own use of analytical structures.

Using the analytical structure for planning

Communication involves much more than just reasoning, and that is why we do not usually communicate via diagrams and lists of claims. But, that said, when we want to express our arguments and explanations clearly and effectively, we need to think carefully about the analytical structure that lies behind the narrative expression of reasoning. It is hard to recover this structure precisely from what you read because authors themselves are often not in control of their reasoning. It is also tricky simultaneously to write a narrative flow and reason analytically. So, before we write, we should *plan* our work on the basis of the reasoning that we wish to 'embed' within our written expression. A very effective way to do this planning is to use the analytical structure format. And, by properly planning our work, we will dramatically improve the quality and readability of our written and oral communication.

How do we develop an analytical structure format? First of all, start thinking about structure and the logical connections between your ideas, rather than how you will actually write them.

1   Decide what your conclusion will be. Write this claim out carefully, expressing exactly what you mean. Number it '1'.

2   Then think about the reasons that you are giving for this conclusion. These reasons must be written as proper claims, this time serving as premises that either explain how that conclusion comes about or show why it should be accepted. Try to keep related premises together, but as the diagram will show these relationships clearly, it is not essential to group them perfectly. Write them out, making sure that you do not use pronouns but express each claim so that it makes sense in and of itself. Number them from '2' onwards. Focus on giving the main reasons for the conclusion at this stage.

3   Begin to draw the diagram to show the relationships between the claims. At this stage the key point is to realise that the symbols you draw in the diagram do not make the reasoning. They are, instead, a representation of the implied links that come from the way you have constructed your claims. Use the line underneath a group of related premises; use the arrow to show a premise-to-conclusion relationship.

4   Stop and think: are you missing any claims? do you need more premises? have you got the relationships the way you want them to be?

5   Make changes if required, adding claims and redrawing the diagram if need be. If necessary, repeat step 4.

Here are five important points to remember when doing this process:

i   Each claim must stand on its own. Do not include pronouns that refer to nouns elsewhere in the argument. Thus, 'Illegal immigrants are treated badly in Australia' is a well-written claim, whereas 'They are treated badly in Australia' is not—who are the 'they' referred to here?

ii   Do not include signals of reasoning in claims: 'Therefore illegal immigrants are treated badly in Australia' is not a proper claim—the word 'therefore' does not belong since the *diagram* will show that this claim is the conclusion.

iii Each claim must imply links to other claims which, when added together, show the reasoning. 'Refugees are treated badly in Australia' and 'Australia violates international human rights treaties' don't connect with one another unless there are other claims. The word Australia appears in both, but other claims involving internal connections between, say, refugees and international human rights must also be included.

iv   You cannot use the symbols (the line and arrow) for just any purpose. Simply drawing extra arrows or lines does not work: the relationships signalled by these symbols must be there already in the claims.

v   Do not be afraid to revise and rewrite. Changing the wording of the claims, moving them around so they fit together logically is the reason you do this process. It is called 'iteration'—you do one version, review it, see if it makes sense, and, if not, you change it and review again.

In later chapters we will explore the subtleties of this process; for now, practise the method as you understand it at the moment.

Exercise 3.5

Choose an issue or topic about which you have some knowledge. If possible, choose a topic that relates to something you are studying; alternatively, use as the basis for your argument some topic that is important to you at the moment. Follow the method outlined above, concentrating on writing clear, single claims and using the diagram to show their interrelation. Then *check the answers* for a discussion of common mistakes that people make. After you have checked for mistakes, try again.

Complex analytical structures

A *simple* argument or explanation is one in which one 'layer' of claims (the premises) links to another claim (the conclusion). In a simple argument the premises are on one level and the conclusion on a second. There may be more than one arrow in the diagram for a simple argument, but each arrow marks out a separate reason that is directly connected to the conclusion. A *complex* argument or explanation (such as that in exercise 3.3), on the other hand, has an analytical structure with more than two levels of connection. The purpose of each layer of claims is to show or explain the claim to which they lead via the arrow. As we will see in chapter 5, such structures make our reasoning more effective.

A complex structure is easy to understand once we realise that it is 'built up' from a group of simple arguments. Here are two simple arguments; the important thing to note is that they share a *common claim*:

1. Australia is a multicultural society.
2. There are people from many different ethnic communities living in Australia.
3. Different ethnic and racial communities contribute different cultures to a society.
4. Government policies and widespread community attitudes encourage these different cultures to mix together and flourish.

and

5. Australia is a tolerant and interesting nation.
6. Multicultural societies show more tolerance towards different groups.
7. Multicultural societies are more interesting than those in which one culture dominates at the expense of other possible cultures.
1. Australia is a multicultural society.

Claim 1 appears twice. In the first example it is being used as the conclusion (and thus will come below claims 2–4 in the diagram). In the second example, claim 1 is functioning as a premise and, thus, goes with the other premises *above* claim 5. Because of the common claim, we can combine the two simple examples to produce a more complex structure, whose relationship would be easily diagrammed. Because the first layer of the diagram does not lead directly to the conclusion, but instead to claim 1, we can call the argument supporting claim 1 a *sub-argument*. It is subsidiary (though still important) to the main argument for claim 5. We just add one diagram to the other, overlapping the common claim:

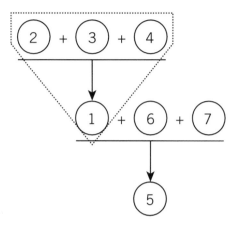

Theoretically, there is no limit to the ways that simple arguments can combine in this manner, but for practical purposes, we may want to limit ourselves to no more than three or four levels of claims, so that the process does not become unwieldy. But it is crucial that we understand the basic idea behind complex structures. Any conclusion is, at base, a claim for which premises are being given. There is nothing to stop that claim from simultaneously serving as a premise itself, which leads to another conclusion.

Exercise 3.6

Let us return to casting to assist our examination of complex structures. To help you understand them, work through the following exercise and then refer to the answers. There is more guidance there about how to cast but, until you have tried it yourself, you will not be able to understand that assistance. You must cast this argument, realising that it has a complex argument structure.

> The current Australian government is, in many ways, challenging the role of the United Nations as a body that promotes action by member nations to maintain and extend human rights within those nations' own jurisdiction. This challenge has a distinct and dangerous consequence for Australia (quite apart from arguments about its dubious morality) because the challenge puts Australia in conflict with most other nations of the world over human rights and Australian trade and foreign relations are likely to suffer in the long run. By definition, this long-term result is dangerous. I believe that the government's role should be to work to avoid danger and, therefore,

I believe the government's current approach to the UN over human rights is incorrect.

Review

In this chapter we have looked at the key process of reasoning: linking. When developing arguments and explanations, we link information expressed as claims. In naturally expressed reasoning, the evidence for this process can be found in certain words and phrases, or even in the arrangement of the claims. But, to understand and control reasoning better, this natural expression is inadequate. It is better to work with a format that shows the analytical structure of reasoning more accurately and consistently. This format may not be suitable for communicating, but it is a tremendous tool for understanding and controlling reasoning in our minds.

The analytical structure of reasoning can be shown by separating an argument or explanation into a list of claims, the interrelationships of which are represented in a diagram using standardised symbols. We can combine a number of simple structures into complex, overlapping, and more effective reasoning. All the intricacies of reasoning can be reduced to a much simpler format. Our initial puzzlement results, not from the complexity of the structured format, but from our unfamiliarity with it. The analytical structure of other people's arguments and explanations can, if we wish, be recovered by 'casting' them into the structured format. However, the analytical structure format is more useful as a tool for planning and thinking about our own reasoning than as a means of direct communication.

CONCEPT CHECK

The following terms and concepts are introduced in this chapter. Before checking in the Glossary, write a short definition of each term:

analytical structure

casting

complex structure

link words

list of claims

narrative flow

simple structure

structure diagram

sub-argument

Review exercise 3

Answer briefly the following questions, giving, where possible, an example in your answer that is different from those used in this book.

- a. What happens to claims when they are linked together so that one gives a reason for the other?
- b. What traces of this linking process can we find in natural language?
- c. What are the symbols in a structure diagram used for?
- d. Are claims, when written in the analytical structure format, expressed differently from those in natural language?
- e. What are the similarities and differences between narrative flow and analytical structure?
- f. How do simple and complex reasoning structures differ?
- g. Can a claim, in one example of reasoning, serve (in relation to a number of claims) as both a conclusion and a premise at the same time?
- h. What advantages and disadvantages are there in learning to use the analytical structure format?

NOTES

1   There is disagreement among philosophers about whether reasoning takes place directly in language, or indirectly in the concepts that are expressed through language. For the purposes of this book, I will take the second position. Of course, if an argument is well written, then the indirect structure should be very clear. However, such clarity is rare in most commonplace language.

2   While I focus on analysis in this book, I do not wish to understate the importance of clear written expression. For more information, consult any of the many good books on written communication that are available.

3   The casting method is commonly used in reasoning textbooks. It was developed principally by Michael Scriven. For an excellent, in-depth look at casting, see J. Rudinow and V. Barry, *Invitation to Critical Thinking*, Wadsworth, Belmont, CA, 2003.

4

Understanding the Links between Claims

Linking claims involves two distinct processes, as signalled by the + and ↓ symbols used in analytical structure diagrams. The first process involves connections between premises and other premises; the second between premises and a conclusion. We must explore these links in more detail in order to understand, first, the analysis that lies behind such connections and, second, how to represent them accurately in the analytical structure format. Of course, in practice, the process of representation often allows us to clarify what we are thinking.

This chapter will cover three main issues:

1 We will look at the way premises almost always work with other premises in providing a reason for a conclusion. What we think of as 'a reason' may, in the analytical structure, require many claims to express all its complexities. These claims add together to form a chain of dependent premises.

2 We will extend this discussion by exploring the way in which, within a group of premises, there can be a premise that links the rest of the premises to the conclusions, and/or a premise that states a definition, making the other premises explicable.

3 We will look at the way links are made between premises and conclusions to better understand the process of making premises support a conclusion.

Dependent premises

Using a group of premises

A 'reason' for a conclusion usually involves many complex ideas. It will probably require more than one premise to express all of these ideas. All such premises relating to a particular 'reason' are *dependent* on one another and thus are shown, in the diagram, as being linked along the same line. Dependency involves one of the key qualities of claims that we looked at in chapter 2: that within a single claim there is an internal connection between two (and, occasionally, more than two) ideas.

In the following claim, the two component parts are (a) and (b):

The Internet (a) has greatly increased the amount of information readily available to researchers (b).

Imagine we are using it to argue for another claim:

The Internet (a) has increased the amount of work that researchers need to do (c).

The first claim only relates to the conclusion via a third claim:

The more information available to researchers (b), the more work they must do (c).

By adding these two claims together, the internal connection between the Internet and more information (a–b) is combined with the connection between more information and more work (b–c) to establish the conclusion's claim that the Internet leads to more work (a–c). The significance of these two premises working together is clear: most people would assume that the *likely* conclusion to a claim that 'The Internet has greatly increased the amount of information readily available to researchers' is that it has made their job *easier*; only by combining premises can we support the opposite view.

Here is another example, this time written in the analytical structure format:

1. Australia's natural environment should be protected.
2. The Australian natural environment is very beautiful.
3. Beautiful natural environments make a country a popular site for international tourism.
4. International tourism is very beneficial to a nation's economy.
5. If something is of benefit to the national economy, then it should be protected.

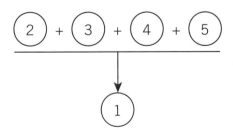

If you look carefully, you will see that, *individually*, none of the premises support the conclusion. How, for example, does a claim about the economic benefits of tourism help us to accept that Australia's natural environment should be protected? It does not, unless it is combined with all the other premises. In adding all four premises together in this manner, there is a process of *cross-linking* going on, in which a connection between two ideas in one claim is extended to a third idea via another claim, and so on, through to the conclusion. This argument is giving one reason—regarding economic benefit—for protecting the Australian environment. The way this reason leads to the conclusion is too complex, however, to be handled by just one or two premises. Instead, to make sure that the relationship of economics to the environment is made clear, four premises are added together in a group.

Exercise 4.1

Write two arguments or explanations (expressed as a list of claims) that match the following generic argument structure. Choose issues about which you have some knowledge or that are important to you at the moment.

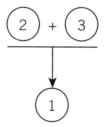

Using independent premises

There is nothing in the analytical structure as such that prevents us from using single, independent premises where each premise offers a reason for the conclusion that is *independent* of other premises. Here is another version of the example about the environment, but this time none of the premises are dependent on one another. Note the three arrows, one for each 'reason', in the diagram.

1. Australia's natural environment should be protected.
2. Environmental protection improves the quality of life for all Australians.
3. Protecting the natural environment will benefit the economy.
4. If Australia's natural environment is looked after, then other countries might follow our example.

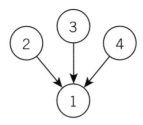

While, obviously, these three reasons are broadly concerned with the same issue, in this argument they are offered independently: no one claim needs any of the others for the argument to make sense. I could, quite legitimately, find out that claim 3 is wrong and yet still be convinced by claims 2 and 4 to accept claim 1. In a dependent chain, if one of the three claims were to 'fall out' in this way, then the entire reason expressed by that chain would be invalidated.

Now compare the previous example to the following variation on our argument, which demonstrates how to use, in one analytical structure, a combination of dependent and independent premises:

1. Australia's natural environment should be protected.
2. Protecting the natural environment will encourage tourism.
3. Increased tourism will benefit the economy.
4. Environmental protection improves the quality of life for all Australians.
5. If Australia's natural environment is looked after, then other countries might follow our example.
6. It would be very good if other countries also protected their natural environments.

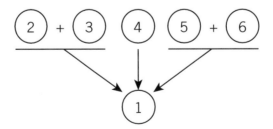

Exercise 4.2

Write two arguments or explanations (expressed as a list of claims) that match the following generic argument structure. Choose issues about which you have some knowledge or that are important to you at the moment.

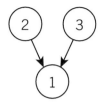

The weakness of independent premises

Independent premises are easier to generate, because we can quickly think of a reason for our conclusion and then jump to expressing it as a single claim. But the resulting independent premises are not strong. They reflect either a lack of insight into the complexity of (most) problems or a failure to recognise that our audience may not be as clever as us at grasping these complexities implicitly. Indeed, there are no genuinely independent premises. What we tend to think of initially as being a single, independent premise is often two (or more) dependent claims; alternatively it may well be a single claim, but one that is dependent on another claim, which we have failed to recognise.

In the following argument, claims 2 and 3 are offered as independent premises:

1. Australia's natural environment should be protected.
2. Tourism will benefit the economy.
3. Environmental protection improves the quality of life for all Australians, which is something we all want.

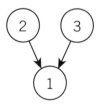

However, claim 2 only supports the conclusion when it is read together with the implied (that is, unstated) premise that:

4. Protecting the natural environment will make Australia a popular tourist destination.

Claim 3 is, when we look closely, a clever way of adding together, in written form, two dependent claims:

3. Environmental protection improves the quality of life for all Australians.

5. All Australians want to improve their quality of life.

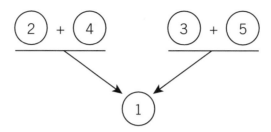

In technical terms, these 'extra' premises explicitly state the necessary cross-linking between the claims' internal connections. More generally, the premises make clear implied information, which in the original argument would have had to be inferred by its audience for it to make sense. In other words, adding these premises moves the information they contain from the implied context to the actual text. In practice, we can produce and use analytical structures with in-dependent premises, but it is rare that these structures will be well thought out and careful. They are, more usually, a sign that we have not explicitly considered some further connection that should be shown in the analytical structure as a chain of dependent premises. We will return to this issue in chapter 6, where we consider how independent premises can only work effectively when their audience can readily supply the hidden, implied extra premises on which they are dependent.

Special functions of premises

In the groups of premises that we have explored in the first section of this chapter, not all premises will perform the same function. Basically, there are three functions for a premise: to make a substantive point, to provide a framework by which substantive premises can be shown to relate to the conclusion, or to define a term in such a way that premises make sense. We will now look in detail at the latter two, special functions of premises.

Premises that provide a framework

When premises combine to form one reason, they usually perform different functions: each premise provides one part of the reason, but is a different type of component. Very often, one claim in particular in a chain of dependent premises will serve a special role in supporting the conclusion. Consider the following argument:

1. Australia's education system should be properly funded by the government.

2. Australia's education system is vital to the future well-being of the nation.
3. If something is vital to the future well-being of the nation, then it should be properly funded by the government.

The premises, claims 2 and 3, are dependent on one another. But each performs a different function as they work together to establish the conclusion. Claim 2 is about a specific item ('Australia's education system'); claim 3, in contrast, is much more general ('something vital to the future well-being of the nation').

I could change the specific focus of the argument, and yet this general claim would remain the same:

1. Australia's defence forces should be properly funded by the government.
2. Australia's defence forces are vital to the future well-being of the nation.
3. If something is vital to the future well-being of the nation, then it should be properly funded by the government.

Although the substance of the argument has changed, claim 3 remains the same. This situation prompts us to ask what task claim 3 is performing in each of these arguments. Through the cross-linking of ideas within each claim, claim 3 is showing why it is that the specific premise stated should give rise to the particular conclusion. In effect, claim 3 answers the implicit question 'why does the first premise lead me to the conclusion?'. We can call claims that function like claim 3 'framing premises'.

A framing premise shows how or why a particular case or piece of evidence relates to the conclusion, usually by claiming that there is some 'general rule' guiding what to do in the sort of case raised by the other premise(s). A 'reason' will, almost always, consist of at least two premises performing two different functions. One or more premises function to give some important information or evidence that, on its own, is not necessarily related to the conclusion; another premise gives the framework that shows why the information given does indeed lead to the conclusion. The precise function of a framing premise, however, cannot be determined in isolation. It is always dependent on the way in which the other premises are trying to establish the conclusion. The relationship between a premise and another premise, then, can only be made by also thinking about the relationship between *all* the premises and the conclusion. Smart thinking is only possible when we recognise the frameworks on which we and others rely.

Exercise 4.3

Identify the framing premises in the following natural arguments (the conclusion is italicised, but you will need to identify the premises and think about how they relate to one another and to the conclusion). Then go back to the arguments you wrote in exercise 4.2: what framing premises should be added to the premises you have already written?

a. Theresa is ill today, and as a result, *she is off work*. I mean, if one is sick, then one should not come to work.

b. When the voters elect politicians, they are, essentially, placing their trust in those politicians. Corrupt politicians have abused the public's trust in them, and when someone abuses your trust, *they should be punished*. That is why corrupt politicians should be sent to jail.

c. All human life is worth protecting, and capital punishment involves taking a human life. Hence *we should oppose capital punishment*.

Premises that provide a definition

In a dependent chain, we sometimes need to include a premise that provides a definition. Definitions tell the audience the meaning of a particular word or phrase found in the other premises and/or conclusion. Definitions are only meaningful in concert with the other claims in the argument or explanation (the ones that actually use the term being defined by the definition). There is little value in simply giving a definition for its own sake; it must be linked in with other premises that depend on that definition. For example:

1. Australians are likely to win more Academy Awards in future.
2. 'Australians' means actors, writers, directors, and so on who have lived and worked in Australia, even if they now live overseas.
3. Australians are increasingly involved in making successful films.
4. Successful films attract the most Academy Award nominations.

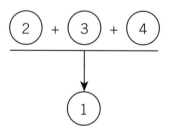

Claim 2 provides the definition. It is necessary to give it in this argument because many people might imagine that 'Australians' means people actually living and working in Australia, whereas the person making this argument is simply talking about a more general category of Australians (for example, the actor Nicole Kidman or the director Bruce Beresford). Claim 2 is only meaningful as a definition because of the way it relates to the other claims.

Definitions are often crucial in reasoning. While many words that we use are 'obvious' in their meaning, others are more complex. Sometimes we want to use words that have a 'common-sense' meaning that is different from the meaning we want to convey in our own argument or explanation (like 'claim' in chapter 2). Good definitions ensure that the other premises relying on a definition can be understood by our audiences when, without the definition, there would be a risk of the premises being misinterpreted. There are four types of definition. Here are some examples:

By 'regulate the free market' I mean:

- action taken by the government such as requiring that accounts be lodged with the Australian Securities and Investments Commission
- something like placing a speed-limiting device on an engine to stop it going too fast
- government actions requiring businesses to perform according to policy rather than market forces
- the opposite of letting innumerable individual decisions about demand and supply determine market interactions.

The first case is a definition *by example*. Such definitions are useful only where the audience will understand the connection between the general definition and specific situation in the example. In the second case, the definition becomes clear via a *comparison* to a similar situation; these definitions are very useful where the intended audience does not know enough about the topic to be given an example but can, through an appropriate comparison, draw upon their knowledge of other topics. The third case gives an *analytic* definition, which uses many words to define some smaller phrase. Here the advantage is that you do not need to keep repeating the longer and more precise definition; instead you can rely on the smaller phrase. The final definition is by *negation*, in which a term's definition is established simply by saying what it is not.

Exercise 4.4

Use each of the four methods to provide a definition for the phrase 'studying critical thinking' in the claim 'studying critical thinking should be part of all university curricula'.

The link from premises to conclusion

In chapter 2, we identified a number of properties of claims that help us not only to determine what a claim is, but also then to write them properly. We have already seen how, in forming groups of dependent premises, what makes these groups work are the similarities and differences in the way we can form claims with these internal connections. We will in this section continue to look at this property of claims, as well as return to a consideration of questions of scope and certainty, and also of value judgment so as to learn better how to make a good link from premises to conclusion. In this section, I will try to model for you the process of writing an argument in the analytical structure format so that you can see how understanding the links between claims also depends on understanding what those claims are saying.

The importance of internal connections

Let's begin by thinking about the following simple claim, which we will use as our conclusion: 'Australia is a good country in which to live'. Now the reason I am asserting this conclusion is that I believe 'Countries that permit freedom of religious expression are good places to live'. So, in theory I could create a structure like this:

1. Australia is a good country in which to live.
2. Countries that permit freedom of religious expression are good places to live.

My knowledge that independent premises are a sign that another, dependent premise is needed cues me to think 'what is missing here?'. The answer comes from the fact that claims 1 and 2 both share the same predicate (good places to live) but have a different subjects: *Australia* (1) and *Countries that permit freedom of religious expression* (2). While it might seem obvious, the problem here is that you cannot move from claim 2 to claim 1 logically without providing an additional claim in which the two different subjects in claims 1 and 2 are themselves placed in a relationship. Such a claim would be 'Australia permits freedom of religious expression'. Thus, by thinking about the internal connections of the claim that is my conclusion, and the first premise I thought of, I have identified an extra premise that is needed in my analytical structure, which now looks like this:

1. Australia is a good country in which to live.
2. Countries that permit freedom of religious expression are good places to live.
3. Australia permits freedom of religious expression.

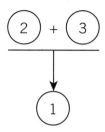

Let us consider another example: I know that Australia has no laws that forbid any religion, and that, by and large, the people who live in Australia let others practise their religions peacefully, even if they do not agree with them. These in fact are the reasons why I had assumed it was obvious that 'Australia permits freedom of religious expression'. But we should not assume our readers know this, or that we are in fact right: we better write in those ideas to make sure the logic is correct. So, now, I am constructing a different argument:

3. Australia permits freedom of religious expression.
4. Australia has no laws that forbid any religion.
5. The people who live in Australia let others practise their religions peacefully even if they do not agree with those religions.

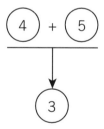

But once again, I can see there is something missing, because of internal connections. The conclusion has, as its predicate, 'freedom of religious expression'. But this term in the argument is not mentioned in either of the two premises, 4 and 5. Hence, I have not yet represented accurately what I am thinking. I should add a claim which will function as a framing premise, and incidentally is an example of the value of the super-claim that has the if/then form: 'If a country has no laws against individual religions and the people of that country do not object to any religious practices, then freedom of religious expression exists in that country'.

3. Australia permits freedom of religious expression.
4. Australia has no laws that forbid any religion.
5. The people who live in Australia let others practise their religions peacefully even if they do not agree with those religions.
6. If a country has no laws against individual religions and the people of

that country do not object to any religious practices, then freedom of religious expression exists in that country.

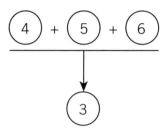

As we can see here, the very fact that you could probably guess what was missing is a sign that the pattern of interconnections in premises and conclusions is important: we are able, often, to see what is missing but should, always, make sure that it is written in explicitly when we are constructing these claim/diagram structures.

Making a real connection

There are times when people make the mistake of *circular reasoning*: that is, they provide a premise or premises that are, effectively, the same as the conclusion. A very obvious example is 'I have failed my exams because I have failed my exams'. No one is foolish enough to actually use such an example. However, we can use different words to say the same thing. Hence, sometimes, people argue in ways that are circular because they present as their conclusion a claim that is the same, logically, as their premise, even though the wording is different. For example 'Socialism is not a workable economic system, because an economic system in which the means of production is collectively owned cannot work' is circular because the claim 'Socialism is not a workable economic system' means the same thing as 'an economic system in which the means of production is collectively owned cannot work'—you can substitute the word 'socialism' for 'an economic system in which the means of production is collectively owned' and not change the meaning of the second claim.

When making your link from premise to conclusion you are relying upon the internal connection between subject and the predicate in the conclusion claim, but you must not have the same connection in a single premise. Instead, you must have the separate elements of the conclusion (the subject; and the predicate) each appearing in *different* claims that serve as premises. Basically, you can only use a claim once within its own argument, not twice; but the constituent components of each claim can appear (and indeed should appear) more than once.

Covering scope and certainty

We also know that claims always imply or state their scope and certainty and attention to this point will permit us to avoid one of the great errors in reasoning:

the *sweeping generalisation*. Often people will make a conclusion that is far too general, or definitive for the reasons they are presenting to support it. An example would be: 'Australia has a good education system with strong programs to teach literacy, and thus all Australians know how to read and write.' It is true that Australia has a good education system with such programs but it is not true, consequentially, that *all* Australians know how to read and write. First, some Australians have learning difficulties or other impairments that prevent them from benefiting from those programs; a few Australians—usually those from disadvantaged backgrounds—face problems in attending school, being able to function effectively there, and so on that again vitiate the impact of those programs. But, logically, the mistake made here is that the scope and certainty of the conclusion is not in step with the scope and certainty of the premise. Therefore when making the link between premises and conclusion, we need to align the scope and certainty so that one can support the other. A better argument would be: 'Australia has a good education system with strong programs to teach literacy, and thus it is *very likely* that Australians will leave school knowing how to read and write'. The change is in the claim that serves as the conclusion: but the consequence of the change is in fact to strengthen the link between the claims.

Thinking about values

I argued above that 'Australia is a good country in which to live', a claim that is obviously making a value judgment. Let us assume, for a moment, that my initial thought as to why this claim is true was 'Australia permits freedom of religious expression'. The mistake here of just having one premise is compounded by the fact that this premise does not make an explicit value judgment and thus suggests something is very wrong with my thinking. Returning to the example above, we can see that part of the job done by the claim 'Countries that permit freedom of religious expression are good places to live' is to place in the premises a claim that, like the conclusion, also asserts a value judgment.

Here is another example concerning value judgments:

1. Ian will be imprisoned.
2. Ian has been convicted of defrauding Michael.
3. The penalty for someone convicted of fraud is imprisonment.

In this analytical structure, the conclusion does not make a value judgment—it does not explicitly state that Ian should or should not be imprisoned. It simply predicts the future based on the premises given. But imagine the argument is concluding 'It is right that Ian should be imprisoned': the premises 2 and 3 do not, in this case, support the conclusion because there is no value judgment there. We would have to add a premise such as 'The penalty of imprisonment for the crime of fraud is a good penalty' to make the structure logical. Of course, the value of being accurate like this is to expose the need for an argument to support this added premise. While it is probably not necessary, in most everyday arguments, to prove Ian's conviction, or that the penalty is imprisonment (these claims, while not self-evident, are reasonably straightforward), I can imagine some situations in which we might want to dispute the rightness of that penalty.

Exercise 4.5

In the following complex argument, identify how the wording of the claims helps you to see the logic of the five arrows which represent the movement from premise to conclusion.

1. Ian should be jailed for between three and six months for assaulting Michael.
2. Ian threatened to attack Michael.
3. By law, threatening to attack someone is known as 'assault'.
4. Ian assaulted Michael.
5. A recent survey of 200 assault victims found that, for over 150 of them, the assault adversely affected their lives for between three and six months after the incident.
6. In most cases of assault, victims suffer for at least three months after the actual assault has ended.
7. Michael will most likely be adversely affected by the assault for at least three months.
8. Michael was relaxed and happy before the assault.
9. Now, after the assault, Michael is depressed and fearful.
10. Nothing other than the assault has happened to Michael that would cause him to be depressed and fearful.
11. Ian's assault on Michael has caused him to be depressed and fearful.
12. If Michael is suffering fear and depression, then it is only right that Ian suffer similarly for a similar period of time.
13. Imprisonment is the only way in which suffering similar to that of Michael's can be inflicted on Ian.

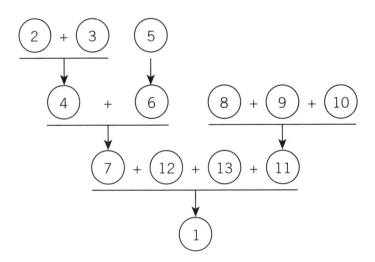

Review

In this chapter we have explored, in considerable depth, how linking between claims works in practice. Links between premises allow us to express the complexities that underlie any summary 'reason'. The key property of claims to be noted here is that a claim contains an internal connection, which then is used as the basis for a chain of external links. Sometimes, a premise functions to frame our argument or define some key term. Sometimes we will encounter a single independent premise, but the connection between this premise and its conclusion is weakened by the absence of explicit claims, which are needed to make that connection clear.

The central idea behind developing our use of dependent premise chains is that, when premises add together [+], they do so in relation to the next logical link, from premises to conclusion [↓]. This arrow is used, in the analytical structure, to represent a relationship that is not just plucked from thin air but which exists implicitly in the claims that are the premises. In making this link, we must be careful that there is a consistency in the scope, certainty, and value between premises and conclusion.

CONCEPT CHECK

The following terms and concepts are introduced in this chapter. Before checking in the Glossary, write a short definition of each term:

circular reasoning

defining premise

dependent premise

framing premise

independent premise

reason

sweeping generalisation

Review exercise 4

Answer briefly the following questions, giving, where possible, an example in your answer that is different from those used in this book:

   a. What distinguishes a 'reason' from a premise?
   b. What is the difference between a dependent premise and an independent premise?

c. Why should we avoid using independent premises?

d. What does a framing premise do?

e. Why are definitions important?

f. How do we use internal connections to make sure we have the right claims in our structure?

g. How do scope and certainty matter in an argument, not just in a single claim?

h. How do conclusions that make value judgments need to be supported by their premises?

5

More Effective
Reasoning I: Better Claims

We have not yet discussed the question of how to reason more effectively. The analytical structure format allows us to see more clearly what we are doing and, thus, gives some basis for improvement. But of itself, the format is not really much help: we must also know how to make our reasoning strong and effective while planning and revising our work. This chapter and the next discuss the ways in which we can avoid errors in reasoning, both initially, in developing our ideas, and then when planning them using the analytical structure format. This format, therefore, can be regarded as a 'checkpoint' at which we can stop and evaluate the strengths and weaknesses of our own arguments and explanations, and then improve them, before fully expressing them in a narrative flow. Remember, the analytical structure itself does not 'make' the reasoning work. It is simply a way of putting your ideas on paper, logically, so you can check and revise them.

This chapter will cover two main areas:

1   We will learn that the claims in our arguments and explanations need to be well formed. A well-formed claim clearly states what it means in a way that allows its truth to be evaluated. A poorly formed claim may or may not truly state something about the world, but its weakness is that we cannot *judge* its truth.
2   We will look at well-founded claims. Such claims are likely to be accepted as true by people reading or hearing them. As we might expect, we need to be sure that the claims we are using are true. However, an effective argument is based as much, if not more, on whether such claims are demonstrably true. Poorly founded claims may

be well formed, but they make claims about the world that our audience finds hard to accept precisely because they appear to have no foundation.

Well-formed claims
Writing clear claims

Smart thinking requires, first of all, that our claims be well formed. Before we even think about how the links between claims might develop—and before we even consider whether or not our claims are acceptable—we need to write or speak clear claims. While this task is similar to all clear writing or speaking, it is not exactly the same. Some of the rules of narrative exposition (such as not repeating words too frequently, the proper use of clauses within sentences, and so on) do not apply at this stage. Most of these rules generate implied links between clauses and sentences; but since your analytical diagram clearly shows these links, we do not need to complicate the claims in this way. Remember, the analytical structure format is designed first and foremost for planning; the good exposition will come later.

So, the primary aim in writing well-formed claims in an analytical structure format is to make each a separate statement that contains all the information necessary for it to express what we mean. The very act of writing the claim carefully will, of itself, help us to understand better what it means. For example, the claim 'Violence against indigenous Australians is wrong' is unclear and vague—even though we would all agree with the sentiment, it is not a 'good' claim. If it is rewritten (for example, to read 'Violence against indigenous Australians by white settlers colonising Australia had and continues to have a negative effect on the moral order of the nation'), then the claim is not as easy to read but clearly shows the meaning of the claim, ready for linking analytically to other claims.

Even at this first stage, as we put together our claims as the basis for our text, we cannot avoid the role of context. The meaning of every word we use is not a fixed absolute, but a socially and culturally constructed convention. By this I mean that the meaning of a word is always determined in relation to all the other words and meanings that are in use within a particular society.[1] Though, for most purposes, the words (and hence the claims) we use seem to be clear in what they mean, we can never simply assume that our audience will always grasp our exact meaning. In particular, while the surface meanings of various words are usually commonly accepted, the connotations (or hidden implications and understandings) of words can vary subtly between different groups of people.

For example, many people in Cuba (still governed within a Marxist system) would not consider the USA a democracy, since people in the USA do not have equal access to education, health, and welfare, whereas in Cuba they do (and thus

Cuba is a democracy). An American would probably regard Cuba as undemocratic in that it only has one political party—the Communist Party—whereas the USA has two major parties. A Cuban might respond by pointing out that the Democrat and Republican parties in the USA are so similar that there is little choice between them. Obviously our hypothetical American and Cuban debaters have different definitions of democracy. Yet, if we asked them to spell out their definition, they might both respond by saying the same things: 'all people have the right to vote'; 'all people are equal'; and so on. The meaning of the word 'democracy' simply depends on *more* words, which themselves require definition. (What do we mean by 'all people', for example? In the USA, most poor African-American and Hispanic citizens do not vote because they believe it will not change the system that, by and large, has failed to benefit them. Do they fall within the definition 'all people'?)

Hence, writing well-formed claims will always require some consideration of both the surface and hidden meanings of the words from which these claims are constructed—meanings that are created differently in different contexts. Connotations can never be controlled completely. We could try to use 'definitions', but definitions themselves give rise to even more connotations (since they, too, are made up of words). One trick is to align your choice of words with the understanding of the intended *audience* so that you can be confident that what *you* mean will be reasonably similar to what your audience might think. And, to be even safer, you can actually discuss possible conflicts of connotations. Alternatively, you can establish (to a large extent) the interpretive context within which you want the meaning of your words to emerge. Either way, you need to consider the possible interpretive contexts that affect your choice of words.

Controlling the key properties of claims

Because a claim makes an internal connection between two ideas, we need to make sure that this connection is expressed as we want it to be. Again, by writing carefully, we also improve our 'analysis' of the issues. Look at the following claims:

a.   Many colonial Australian settlers took part in military-style operations against indigenous Australians throughout the nineteenth century, in different parts of the country.

b.   The violent conflict between white settlers and indigenous Australians was wrong.

c.   Some Australian political and religious leaders in the nineteenth century wrote at the time that the violent conflict between white settlers and indigenous Australians was wrong.

d.   Historians should continue to debate the extent to which indigenous Australians fought back against the process of European settlement.

e   If Australians do not come to terms with the violent events associated with the nation's colonial foundation, then Australians today will continue to experience unease and guilt about race relations with indigenous Australians.

f. The history of the war against indigenous Australians continues to be a political issue in the current era.

These claims might all concern the broad topic of the violence attendant on the arrival of European settlers in the country we now call Australia, but in each case, the primary focus of the claim is different.

- Claim **a** is about the actions of white settlers in the nineteenth century.
- Claim **b** is about the conflict between settlers and indigenous Australians.
- Claim **c** identifies the views of some Australian political and religious leaders in the nineteenth century.
- Claim **d** concerns what historians should be debating.
- Claim **e** predicts the consequences that will flow from some action concerning the history of violence in Australia, which may or may not happen (as indicated by the 'if').
- Claim **f** concerns the current status of the history of the war against indigenous Australians, about which many of the other claims might be made.

The differences also show us that there are a variety of different uses for claims. Claims **a** and **b** are *direct* claims, in the first case describing some event and in the second case directly expressing the author's own moral judgment. However, 'Some Australian political and religious leaders in the nineteenth century wrote at the time that the violent conflict between white settlers and indigenous Australians was wrong' is indirect, for it concerns what other people think. There is no indication that the author of the claim either agrees or disagrees with the 'political and religious leaders' who thought this way. Arguments and explanations often require not just our own views on a particular issue, but also our analysis of others' views. We need to make sure that our claims are well formed so that there is no confusion between what we are directly claiming and what we are reporting about other people's views. Claim **e** demonstrates another crucial type of claim, often used in hypothetical reasoning about a possible future event. To argue in this manner does not necessarily imply that the effect (the 'then' part of the claim) has happened, but simply that it *probably will* happen in the future. It may even be part of an argument aimed at stopping some action from happening. We might also find such hypothetical elements in claims such as 'Let us assume for a moment that the violence between whites and indigenous Australians did not occur': such claims do not propose that it did not happen, but simply develop a hypothetical situation that might enable a clearer analysis to proceed. The key point here is to recognise that claims can say and do all sorts of things, and if you are not careful in how you write them, then they will provide a very weak foundation for your analytical structure.

Making claims also involves deciding between values and descriptions. We can think about the six examples just given from this perspective: claims **a**, **c**, and **f** describe some state of affairs; whereas claims **b** and **d** make explicit value judgments about the goodness or otherwise of some state of affairs; claim **e** sits uneasily between these two alternatives; and while claim **e** appears to be free of values, most of us would probably see in it some *implicit* value judgment, probably because of the implication in the first half of the claim that we should do the opposite of the 'if'. Yet it is unlikely that we will ever be able to write many claims that are completely free of value judgments. An individual claim may be descriptive, but it can only be understood in relation to other claims and other words. What appears, to us, to be a description will, necessarily, appear to others as a judgment of value. For many years, the word 'violence' was never used to describe white settlement in Australia. Thus, when historians began to uncover the evidence of violence, their claims appeared in comparison to be distinctly value-laden. So we must simply be aware of the value judgments in our claims in order to understand what we are saying.

Claims always involve, implicitly or explicitly, some statement of the scope and certainty of the information they contain. Well-formed claims always state their scope and certainty explicitly. For example, 'Australians took part in military-style operations against indigenous Australians' is unclear. How many—all of them, some, a few? Where did this occur? And for how long? Whatever you wish to say about this issue (and there are competing views among historians), a well-formed claim should try to make clear what you are asserting. Hence, (for example) 'Many colonial Australian settlers took part in military-style operations against indigenous Australians throughout the nineteenth century, in different parts of the country' is a better-formed claim.

Exercise 5.1

Identify, in the following claims: (i) the two components of the claims, paying particular attention to claims that state someone else's views or that employ the 'if ... then' form; (ii) the value judgments that some of them are making (explicitly or implicitly); (iii) the explicit or implicit markers of scope and certainty that are essential to the claim's proper functioning; and (iv) any words that might appear to have interesting connotations.

   a. Some years ago, the Northern Territory passed legislation allowing some people to commit voluntary euthanasia.
   b. Most religious leaders at the time, and now, claim that legislation permitting voluntary euthanasia is immoral.
   c. If a state government passed voluntary euthanasia laws, then the Federal Government would not be able to stop that legislation in the same way that it did for the Northern Territory.
   d. Several terminally ill people were reported in the media at the time as saying they were moving to the Northern Territory.

e. I imagine that if another state or territory were to pass similar laws, then media reporting of the legislation would be very extensive.

f. Some politicians argued that media reporting at the time of the Northern Territory legislation encouraged some terminally ill people to move there.

Well-founded claims

The problem of 'true' claims

A claim, whether it is a conclusion or a premise, has one essential property: that it claims to be a true statement (either actual or possible—what is or what ought to be). Hence, while claims must first be well formed, so that we can express this state of affairs precisely, claims must also be well founded, so that their truth is not too easily called into question. If I were to say, 'This book will totally change your life!', you would probably not accept this claim, because as it stands, this claim is *unfounded* (not based on believable intellectual foundations) and is thus of doubtful truth.

The whole purpose of using reasoning is, in fact, to give foundations (via the premises) for the conclusion, to show that it is acceptable, or to establish an acceptable explanation of it. Obviously, then, the 'well-foundedness' of the premises becomes equally (if not more) important than the well-foundedness of the conclusion. How can an audience assess our conclusion except by first considering the premises? Indeed, for any claim to be well founded, whether it be conclusion or premise, there must be some reason(s) for the audience accepting it. Every claim, in this sense, must be treated as a conclusion in need of premises. Every argument or explanation in which we use premises to prove a conclusion depends, therefore, on *other* arguments or explanations, which establish those premises. We have seen this situation in some of the examples in previous chapters, in which a conclusion is reached only after a series of arguments (arranged in a complex structure) have been developed.

Here is an example:

1. Australia is a good country in which to live.
2. Countries that permit freedom of religious expression are good places to live.
3. Australia permits freedom of religious expression.
4. Australia has no laws that forbid any religion.
5. The people who live in Australia let others practise their religions peacefully even if they do not agree with those religions.
6. If a country has no laws against individual religions and the people of that country do not object to any religious practices, then freedom of religious expression exists in that country.

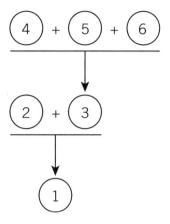

Claim 3 is being supported by an argument provided by 4, 5, and 6. Of course, we might also ask what claims should be there to support 4, 5, and 6.

Theoretically, if all claims must be supported by reasons, then there would be no guaranteed starting points to any process of reasoning. In structural terms, every claim that we use at the top of a diagram would always appear to need a further argument above it to show why that claim was acceptable. In such a situation, reasoning would be impossible—the very ideas of 'foundations' would go out the window.

In practice it is much simpler. We take for granted that many, perhaps most, claims we use are *not* going to have explicit reasons, but instead will be presented as being 'self-evidently' acceptable (that is, without any evidence but themselves). Societies, and particular knowledge groups (such as a profession or academic discipline) within them, have many agreed conventions and assumptions that short-circuit the need to justify in detail every single claim they use; there are also many legitimate, accepted starting points provided by claims for which no further reasoning is required (because the argument for them exists implicitly in the surrounding context of knowledge and audience).

Now, strictly speaking, very few claims are *logically* self-evident. One that is, for example, would be the claim that 'Either you are pregnant or you are not'. No matter *who* this claim is applied to, no matter what the situation, it is self-evident. There is no category of 'a little bit pregnant'. But such claims are actually quite rare: their function in argument is simply to define a term in such a manner as to make clear its exclusivity. Such claims do not actually refer to the world, but to the words we use in the world—the claim 'My sister is pregnant' is not self-evident. However, many claims which are not self-evident are treated *as if* they are self-evident, revealing the social dimensions of reasoning. In the world of strict logic, outside of common practice and normal human interactions, virtually every claim must be supported by evidence; in the everyday world of reasoning, many claims are assumed to be self-evident. They must be regarded as such. There would be no way for reasoning to proceed if we did not make these assumptions of self-evidence.

Arguments begin with claims that are more acceptable (that is, well founded without the need for argument) and move onwards to claims that are less acceptable (that is, most in need of an argument to justify them). An explanation may end with a well-known claim as its conclusion but should begin with the more readily accepted explanatory premises. Not only must the starting claims be well founded as far as we are concerned, but we also need to be reasonably sure our audience will concur with us. Some claims, perhaps even just one, will need to be presented as self-evidently well founded. But many other claims will only become effective when properly founded by something we do to support them, showing our audience why and how they are well founded. Let us then look at the ways in which we might do this. First of all we will consider why it is that some claims can appear, on their own, as well founded, and then examine two ways in which we can present extra information to our audience to support those claims that cannot stand on their own.

Claims whose truthfulness is not in question

An example of a claim that we might expect to use self-evidently is 'The earth orbits the sun'. But, if we are to be sure that the claims in our arguments and explanations are well founded in the context of their audience, we cannot simply assume that they are self-evident. For example, a group of young children would, probably, need to be convinced that the earth orbited the sun since, just on the basis of their observation, the sun goes around the earth. But, we can assume, a group of adults would not require any such convincing: they will have already come to accept that 'the earth orbits the sun' is a true claim.

The difficulty, of course, is that apart from some obvious claims, such as the example just used, most claims are in doubt to some degree or another, or for some audience or another. And there is another category of claim that poses an even more difficult problem: claims whose truthfulness is not in doubt, *but should be*! Here is an example of this dual dilemma. If someone claimed, without giving a foundation, that 'citizens of Singapore enjoy considerable freedom', then many Australians (and Singaporeans) might doubt the truth of this claim. In doing so, they would be drawing on existing (that is, contextual) knowledge of, say, the limitations of free speech in Singapore, the many restrictions on what one can and cannot do, and the fact that Singapore has always been governed by the same political party since gaining independence from the United Kingdom.

To establish the truth of the claim, its author would have to somehow overcome the audience's initial scepticism. Such a claim might well be true if we understand that freedom can mean both freedom to do some positive act (that is, the freedom to voice critical opinions of the government) and freedom from some negative circumstance (that is, freedom from hunger and poverty). Hence, although the author of the claim is convinced that it is well founded, if the author were to propose that 'citizens of Singapore enjoy considerable freedom' without carefully arguing or explaining what was meant, the audience might well refuse to accept the claim. Equally, people often believe claims about which there is considerable doubt. For example, most Australians would not think twice before accepting that 'citizens of Australia enjoy considerable freedom' was a true claim. In doing so, they would draw on existing knowledge (as in the first example). But, obviously, when we consider the 'negative freedom' definition, we might think that the claim was more doubtful. Such doubts might readily spring to mind for indigenous Australian people, whose capacity to enjoy the positive freedoms of Australian citizenship is seriously constrained by inequities in, for example, housing, health, and employment.

At some point, of course, we have to use claims that, since we are giving no argument or other support for them, are presented as self-evidently true, or that are so widely accepted to be true (by our audience) that they do not require further justification. We must also rely on the fact that, as authors, we are presumed by our audience to have some knowledge about our subject and can thus be 'trusted' to make acceptable claims. (Obviously certain authors—experts, renowned scholars, and so on—can rely on this trust a good deal more than others; such trust is clearly a contextual component of the overall text.) In this way, we are ourselves involved in creating the context in which our reasoning exists.

But we need to consider many other contextual factors so that, in the end result, our self-evident claims do indeed turn out to be acceptable to our audience. We must, in effect, judge in advance the likelihood that someone reading or hearing our reasoning will 'doubt' that a claim is true. If it is possible that this situation will occur, then we must counter this 'doubt' in advance. While the basis for our judgment must include attention to the claim itself, we can only argue and explain the claim effectively if we *also* judge its acceptability in relation to our audience. Finally, more pragmatic issues emerge from a consideration of context: what is expected of your particular argument in terms of length and scope. For example, it is unreasonable (according to most social conventions) to expect most arguments and explanations to contain the level of detail that, for example, we find in lengthy scholarly work. We can adjust our reasoning accordingly by thinking about its context as well as what it actually contains (the text).

Exercise 5.2

Which of the following claims would be regarded as self-evidently true by a general adult audience? In each case, explain your answer:

a. Communism has failed.
b. Television was introduced to Australia in 1956.
c. Australia is a democracy.
d. We should legalise marijuana.

e.   The two main political parties are the Liberal Party of Australia and the Australian Labor Party.
f.   A broken leg requires immediate medical treatment.

Claims supported by authority

Perhaps the most common way of overcoming this 'problem'—the risk that our claims may not be accepted—is to support them by an appeal to authority. This is a very special form of reasoning that, to establish the acceptability of a claim, does not give an argument but makes reference (in one or more ways) to an expert. In this reference, an appeal to authority indirectly points to arguments or explanations that would, if checked, support the claim.

There are many conventional forms of reasoning in which we come across claims supported by authority. Here are some examples (the words that provide the reference to a particular form of authority are italicised):

a.   'Gender and sexual definitions [have] become the focus of intense cultural negotiation' (*Gledhill 1992, p. 201*).
b.   Australian history is marked by considerable conflict and tension over the competing interests of labour and capital (*see Rickard 1992*).
c.   *According to Dr Jane Long, who has studied this topic in detail*, poor women in nineteenth-century England were, by and large, worse off than poor men.
d.   *In my twenty years' experience as a High Court judge*, I have come across few cases as complex as this one.
e.   *I look back on my childhood and recall* that I was always encouraged to ask 'why?' by my parents.
f.   *The experiments I have conducted* show that many cleaning products induce allergic reactions in humans.

You should be reasonably familiar with the type of support offered in claims **a** and **b**. Here the claims are stated and a reference given to the book, chapter, or article from which they are drawn. In the first, the reference is direct: Gledhill's actual words are quoted (and the reference would be given in full in the bibliography). In the second, the reference is indirect: the claim given summarises a discussion in Rickard's book. References such as these acknowledge the source of ideas and evidence, but also provide support for the claims. In effect, they say 'This claim I now make is well founded because it has been previously established by someone else, and here is the reference to that person's work so you can go and check for yourself'. The insistence in academic work on proper referencing is, therefore, not simply a tedious necessity but a significant part of the main purpose of writing: the clear expression of good arguments or explanations.

Claims **c** and **d** are slightly different. They are similar in that the acceptability of the claim in each case is founded on the authority of an expert, but there is no 'source' to check up on. In claim **c**, the authority is that of someone who has studied a subject and is, presumably, an expert on such matters. In claim **d**, the authority comes not from study, but from relevant personal experience—that is, experience that does, in fact, help to establish the claim. Claim **e** provides another significant type of authority: the authority of personal experience in relation to one's own life (one is usually an expert on one's own life, though not always). Claim **f** is different again, and a significant form of authority in most scientific and social science research. As noted above, authors can present claims as being self-evidently true via the audience's trust that they are accurate researchers, investigators, and thinkers. In this case, we simply find an explicit statement that calls upon that trust. But, in each case, the inclusion of some reference to authority functions to support the truthfulness of the claim, and in that respect, there is more similarity than difference between the five examples.

Exercise 5.3

For each of the following, indicate an appropriate authority to whom you might refer if required to establish the foundation of these claims. Remember, you are not reasoning here but are referring to some *source* of reasoning about the claim:

a. Communism has failed.
b. Television was introduced to Australia in 1956.
c. Australia is a democracy.
d. We should legalise marijuana.
e. The two main political parties are the Liberal Party of Australia and the Australian Labor Party.
f. A broken leg requires immediate medical treatment.

Let us at this stage return to the analytical structure format to show how we might represent these calls to authority. First of all, think about the way that the list of claims is designed to express clearly what we mean. Imagine we wish to claim that 'Australian history is marked by considerable conflict and tension over the competing interests of labour and capital' and *use* as support the fact that a competent, respected historian such as John Rickard has also made this claim in his book *Australia: A Cultural History*. We would write:

1. The Australian government should continue to regulate industrial relations practice and policy.
2. Australian history is marked by considerable conflict and tension over the competing industrial interests of labour and capital.
3. Rickard, *Australia: A Cultural History* (1992) asserts claim 2.
4. These conflicts and tensions have been resolved, by and large, by government intervention.
5. It is unlikely that, in future, the conflict that results from the competing industrial interests of labour and capital will decline.

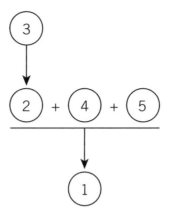

Note that, in this example, we are *not* engaging in an analysis of the fact that Rickard has made this claim. That is why we separate the authority from the substantive claim it is supporting. If we were trying to show why Rickard was right or wrong to make it, then we would combine the claims together and write: 'Rickard has argued that Australian history is marked by considerable conflict and tension over the competing interests of labour and capital'. By doing so, we would be starting to analyse the fact that Rickard has made that argument. In simple use of authority, by contrast, the authority and the claim that is relying on it have the same logical connection as that by which claims prove or show another claim. Hence it is appropriate to diagram the relationship using the arrow.

Claims supported by reasoning

Looking back to the last example, what should we do about claims 4 and 5, for which no clear foundation is offered? Well, rather than allow their foundations to remain implicit, we can argue for claims 4 and 5 in precisely the same way as we are arguing for claim 1, thus developing a complex argument structure. We could, for example, add the following claims to our argument, not to support claim 1 directly but to show why claim 5 was acceptable.

6. Capitalist economies are structured in a way that creates two groups: labour (those employed) and capital (those who do the employing).
7. These two groups will always have different interests.
8. It is highly likely that, in future, Australia will continue to have a capitalist economy.

In the overall argument, claims 6–8 form a subsidiary argument to support claim 5 (one of the main premises in the argument), which in turn helps to explain the conclusion. Claim 5, therefore, serves in two different ways: as a conclusion and a premise. There is no difference in the way that the two arrows operate, nor in the way that the linking between premises operates in either the first or second part of the argument. Hence, all of the next chapter, which discusses in detail the effective construction of links between claims, is applicable to subsidiary arguments, such as the one involving claims 5, 6, 7, and 8, as well as to main arguments, such as that involving claims 2, 4, 5, and 1.

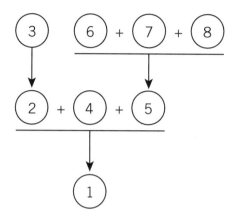

Exercise 5.4

For each of the following, write a brief argument (in analytical structure format) that establishes the acceptability of these claims. In each case, remember that the claims you use in support of the following conclusions should be more self-evident than the conclusions themselves.

a. Communism has failed.
b. Television was introduced to Australia in 1956.
c. Australia is a democracy.
d. We should legalise marijuana.
e. The two main political parties are the Liberal Party of Australia and the Australian Labor Party.
f. A broken leg requires immediate medical treatment.

Review

Claims have certain key properties that we must understand if we are to be effective reasoners. The only way to achieve a level of control over our claims is to make sure that, as we write each claim, we know—at some level—how we are formulating each component properly. Yet we cannot ignore the contextual issues relating to meaning and connotation that will affect others' judgments of how well formed our claims appear to be. Making a well-founded claim involves, at the very least, considering whether we believe it to be true (on the basis of whatever evidence we have, or have seen or read) and then considering whether or not our audiences will believe it to be true. Well-founded claims are not just 'true'; they are *accepted* as true. There are three types of well-founded claims: those that are 'self-evident' (and, in that sense, are their own foundation); those that are founded on a reference to authority or expertise (including one's own 'authority'); and those that are founded (like the conclusion to any argument or explanation) via further reasoning.

CONCEPT CHECK

The following terms and concepts are introduced in this chapter. Before checking in the Glossary, write a short definition of each term:

appeal to authority

effective reasoning

implied premise

modes of analysis

self-evident claim

well-formed claim

well-founded claim

Review exercise 5

Answer briefly the following questions, giving, where possible, an example in your answer that is different from those used in this book:

   a. Why are well-formed claims essential?
   b. What is the role of connotations in thinking about well-formed claims?
   c. What is the difference between claiming 'X happened' and 'Jones has argued that X happened'?
   d. What roles do scope and certainty play in well-formed claims?
   e. Which claims are least likely to be 'self-evident'?
   f. What is the similarity between premise-claims supporting a conclusion and other claims supporting those premises?
   g. How might we 'found' claims so that they are more acceptable?
   h. How can we judge the 'truth' of a claim in trying to communicate our reasoning effectively?

NOTES

1   See Tony Schirato and Susan Yell, *Communication and culture: an introduction*, Sage, London, 2000 for an in-depth treatment of this important issue.

6

More Effective Reasoning II: Better Links

Writing well-formed and well-founded claims is only half the task of effective reasoning. The links between these claims must also be well made if our overall argument or explanation is to be strong. Looking carefully at the links between premises prevents us from making unconscious assumptions about how information is interrelated. We must also check the connections of our premises with their conclusion, making sure they are *relevant* and provide strong support. Otherwise our conclusion will not be acceptable, or the explanation of it will be unconvincing. At each stage, as discussed in chapter 5, we will need to consider the way that the context of our reasoning will affect our judgments about its effectiveness.

In this chapter we will consider three main issues:

1   We look at how effective reasoning requires that we work out the necessary links between dependent premises. Carefully expanding our 'reasons' into a fully expressed chain of premises ensures that our reasoning has depth, so that no important premises remain 'implied' (not explicitly stated).

2   We will consider how relevant premises provide information that does actually bear on the conclusion, whereas irrelevant premises (even if well formed and well founded) do not.

3   We examine the strength of the support that premises provide for a conclusion. As we saw with well-founded claims, judgments of audience expectations and other contextual issues play a central role in making sure our reasoning is effective.

Effective use of dependent premises

Dependent premises providing one reason

A reason for a conclusion is very unlikely to consist in a single claim. No matter how we might state it in short-hand, it is, analytically, a complex interaction of many ideas and implications. The reason must be broken down into a chain of more precise premises. For example, the claim that 'university education should be free for all Australians' might be supported by the reason that 'the economy benefits from a well-educated Australian population'. But is our analysis of the situation clearly expressed in just one statement? Hardly. The conclusion is about universities and free education, while the reason introduces some new ideas: economic benefit and a well-educated population. While the link between these two ideas and the conclusion might seem obvious, the purpose of reasoning is to avoid assuming the 'obvious' by carefully working through the connections between the various ideas in the initial statement of our reason.

Here is how we might do it:

1. University education should be free for all Australians.
2. A well-educated population is more productive at work.
3. Higher productivity at work benefits the economy.
4. If something benefits the economy, then the government should encourage it.
5. The best way for the government to encourage Australians to be well educated is to provide free university education.
6. In our complex technological society, one requires university study in order to be well educated.

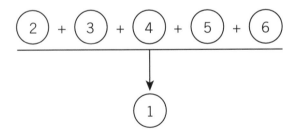

Now turning one reason—'the economy benefits from a well-educated Australian population'—into five separate premises does *not* provide any additional, different reasons. Rather, we have 'unpacked' some of the hidden aspects and implications of *one* reason and shown how they relate to one another.[1] For example, in the initial reason 'well-educated' is not defined. There are many different opinions on what constitutes such an education, and claim 6, a definition, overcomes this source of confusion. Claims 2 and 3 make clear the exact relationship between economic benefit and education. Moreover, by expanding the hidden aspects of our initial reason, we have discovered a key issue: who should pay. No matter how strongly we might believe it, the reason 'education benefits the economy' does not, of itself, mean education's users should not pay. This implication is *not* self-evident. If we want to argue that education should be free, then we must say why. Claims 4 and 5 provide, then, an explication of the idea of *free* education. Note how claim 4, in particular, expresses a clear value judgment: the government should do something. Since the conclusion is a value claim ('education *should* be free'), there must be a premise somewhere that addresses the value judgment involved here.

If we were to provide an additional reason, 'free education is a fundamental democratic right', we need to keep it separate (both in our minds and on paper) from the reason about economic benefit. We would, of course, need to expand this initial reason into a series of dependent premises, but they would occupy a different place in the analytical structure of our argument. We could unpack this additional reason into claims and include them in the format:

7. Free education is a fundamental democratic right.
8. Australia is a democracy.
9. Education includes all levels from primary to tertiary.

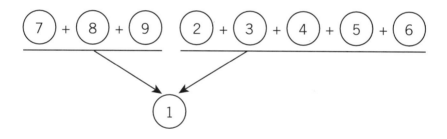

In this process of unpacking or expanding a basic reason for a conclusion, we should carefully distinguish between the *internal complexities* of that statement (which become a series of dependent claims), and any new claims that we introduce to make a dependent claim well founded. One of the claims resulting from our expansion of the economic benefit reason was 'The best way for the government to encourage Australians to be well educated is to provide free university education' (claim 5). We could show why claim 5 was true by including the following claims:

10. Any cost that the government imposes on people attending higher education will probably reduce the numbers attending.
11. If numbers are reduced, then Australians are obviously not being encouraged to attend.

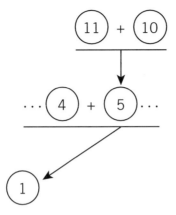

Claims that argue for or explain another claim are always placed *above* them; claims that work together to form one reason are placed *alongside* one another, as a chain of dependent premises. Getting the diagram right doesn't make this happen, it is a way of representing—in a structured format—what is happening in our minds.

We tend to imagine that strong reasoning involves understanding and using a number of different reasons for our conclusion, giving our arguments and explanations intellectual breadth. This view has considerable merit (and we examine it in more detail in the next section), but it does not mean that we can ignore the requirement to argue and explain *in depth*. Learning to 'unpack' what we initially think of as a straightforward, simple reason and to express it as a number of distinct, but dependent, premises is the only way to make sure our reasoning is not too shallow.

For example, in relation to higher education, deep reasoning will bring out the current debate about whether education is vocational (training for employment) or liberal (education for the individual's own life). It would engage with the complex issues of who pays, against a background of reduced government spending and increased personal wealth for some Australians. It would engage with the social purposes of education (education for individual benefit or for social improvement). Each of these issues is worthy of significant argument and explanation in its own right. Such an approach ensures that our reasoning addresses all the issues raised by the conclusion: the meaning of certain words, the values that we are seeking to express, the exact way in which certain situations come about, and so on.

Avoiding implied premises

If, in unpacking our reason and turning it into premises, we leave out a premise that should (analytically speaking) be there, then we have made a serious error. Such a claim would not be 'missing' exactly, but rather would be implied by the connection between the claims that are explicitly stated. That we do often 'leave out' some of these premises is a reflection of the difficulty of thinking deeply enough about complex issues. When we do, it is usually because we have unconsciously assumed some complex relationship that, in fact, needs more open analysis.

Here is an example. Imagine we reasoned that 'The economy is growing strongly at the moment, so employment will also grow strongly'. If we look closely, this explanation does not represent a clear analysis. The first claim puts together two components ('economy' and 'growth'); the second (the conclusion) puts together 'employment' and 'growth'. What has been implied? We do not have to guess because, from the available information, we can infer that the implied claim is a premise that connects 'economy' with 'employment'. Such a premise might be: 'Economic growth is necessarily a cause of employment growth'. And, from this example, we can extract a general rule: when deciding what the implied premise might be, ask 'on what basis, according to what other piece of information, does the stated premise (or premises) provide a reason for accepting the conclusion?'. If the link between the premises and the conclusion is unclear, then there is probably an implied premise.

The original explanation about the economy contains an implied premise because the initial 'reason' had not been unpacked, allowing each *necessary* element to be written as an explicit claim. Failures to expand reasons properly lead to implied premises and reflect assumptions made by the person arguing or explaining, which interfere with smart analysis. Historically, economic growth has caused employment to grow, but as is evidenced by the past decade in Australia, the new shape of capitalist economies in the 1990s and the new century means that this old idea is no longer valid. This mistake—of assuming it is true to say 'economic growth means more jobs'—has been common in recent years. Because the reason was not unpacked properly and the analytical relationship made explicit, the original explanation did not provide a clear opportunity to analyse this assumption and check to see if it was true.

But it is also wrong to rely on implied premises (that is, those that are analytically necessary but have not been clearly stated) even when such premises are true. Look at this example:

> A computer technician is called out to look at a personal computer that is not working very well. The technician knows perfectly well what is wrong: the computer has only got 256 megabytes of random access memory (RAM), and its owner is trying to run programs that require at least 512 megabytes. So, she explains to the customer, 'Your computer is not working well because it only has 256 megabytes of RAM'.

What the technician has done, though, is to rely on the implied premise that 'If you wish to run the programs loaded on this machine, then you must have at least 512 megabytes of RAM'. The relationship between memory, the computer, and the problem is so obvious to the technician that she has not clearly explained it. Yet, the customer may not know enough about computers to 'fill in' or infer the implied premise from the stated explanation. The implied premise here is true. What has been assumed is that the relationship between the premises and the conclusion is obvious. In fact, from the point of view of the customer, it is not, and thus the reasoning used by the technician is ineffective.

By definition, all reasoning depends at some point or another on assumptions that give rise to implied claims. So, practically speaking, effective reasoning does not require that there be *no* implied premises. But it does require that we be well aware of the claims that we do leave out. First, if we do not recognise our own implied premises, then we may fail to judge accurately if they are true or not; second, we may fail to communicate our message to someone else who does not share our assumptions. This last point is particularly important. Our decisions about using implied premises can only be guided by what we expect our audience to know, and what we know, about the context of our reasoning. For example, academic essays and reports are usually designed precisely to test students' abilities to avoid making assumptions, and so, we would not want to leave many implied premises in this context, even though we might assume our audience (the assessors) do know the claims we are making.

Exercise 6.1

Think of two completely separate reasons for each of the following two con-clusions. Write these reasons down, and then analyse their relationship to the conclusion, expanding each into a chain of dependent premises. In the first case, you are explaining why the conclusion is happening; in the second case you are arguing for it to be accepted.

   a.   I am reading a book on reasoning.
   b.   There are considerable benefits to be gained from studying how to think better.

Relevance

What is relevance?

Here is a simple example of relevance and irrelevance concerning the conclusion 'Smith is physically unhealthy':

   a.   Smith has pains in his chest; he coughs a lot and is short of breath walking up stairs. Clearly Smith is physically unhealthy.
   b.   Smith wears green trousers and a pink hat and has no shirt on. Clearly Smith is physically unhealthy.

In argument **a**, the relevance of the premises is clear: they all report physical symptoms that are routinely recognised as evidence of poor health. In the second case, these premises are irrelevant because they give us no indication of physical health. Note that it is impossible to determine the relevance of the premises by themselves: we must look at their relationship to the conclusion. Argument **b** contains a number of irrelevant premises, but if the conclusion were 'Smith has no conventional sense of good dress', then, clearly, the claims about his hat, trousers, and bare chest would be relevant. What determines the easy judgment that **a** is a good argument and **b** is a bad argument is the implied premise 'physical symptoms are relevant evidence from which to induce a conclusion about physical health'. Indeed it is so obvious—in our society, but perhaps not others—that we would be thought odd if we actually explicitly stated that premise.

Relevance is often a major problem in argumentation. Poor arguments regularly report the 'facts' well, and try to draw conclusions from them but do not establish the relevance of the premises given to the conclusion asserted. Poor skills in reasoning, especially not identifying one's assumptions, are one cause. As we considered in chapter 4 one of the functions of premises is, precisely, to establish relevance—not something which all people who use reasoning realise. However it is not just a problem of technique. Often the debates in our society that are most difficult to resolve concern disagreements about whether or not a premise is relevant to a given conclusion. Consider the treatment of people who arrive as refugees in Australia directly, rather than by official routes (so-called 'illegal immigrants'). Politicians who support detention of these people argue that international laws concerning the proper treatment of refugees are not relevant to this class of immigrants because they have arrived illegally. Opponents of detention counter by saying the international laws are relevant. On both sides, there is agreement that there are such laws, and that they do prohibit detention; there is also agreement that people are arriving in this manner. What differs is the judgment as to whether or not the refugees are arriving legally or illegally and, in consequence, whether human rights conventions are or are not relevant.

Issues of relevance are rarely as obvious as the example about Smith and his health that I used at the start of this section. Smart thinking always involves very careful consideration of relevance as distinct from whether or not premises are well founded. To emphasise, relevance of premises is *completely different* from the acceptability of premises. A claim can be true (and thus acceptable), but this quality alone does not necessarily mean it is relevant to the conclusion. For example, it is definitely the case that, as you read these words, the claim 'You are reading this book' is true and acceptable. But is it relevant to the conclusion 'You are going to cook fish for dinner tonight'? No! Hence, in making our arguments and explanations effective, we should not be satisfied simply that our premises are acceptable in themselves: for them to give any support to the conclusion, they must also be relevant to it. So, put simply, a premise is relevant to the conclusion when it provides some basis on which to decide whether or not to accept that conclusion.

Exercise 6.2

To help you to learn about relevance, let us look at some examples. In the following arguments and explanations, decide which premises are relevant to the conclusion (which is italicised in each case):

   a. *Why did the train crash?* The train was going too fast and its brakes were faulty; also, there were many people waiting at the station.

b. Now, first of all, privatisation leads to competition and, when there is competition, prices go down and service improves. People want reduced prices and improved service in the postal system and so *the government postal service should be privatised.*

c. Several politicians have been discovered to have lied in public; many rarely seem to have much knowledge of what their voters want; and generally, politicians get too many benefits. Hence *we should not trust them to make good decisions on our behalf.*

Ensuring premises are relevant

But what if the connection between a premise and a conclusion is not obvious? A crucial smart-thinking skill is the ability to think through how evidence relates to a conclusion, and how apparently irrelevant material does indeed help to prove or establish a conclusion. Making sure premises are relevant to a conclusion requires careful analysis of the possible connections between them. As noted above, the key question is whether or not the premises are concerned with the same issue as the conclusion and, hence, whether they are capable of telling us something about it. A way to check this relationship is to ask, in the case of arguments, 'if this premise were true, would it make the conclusion more likely to be true' or, for explanations, 'if this premise were true, would it make it easier to understand why the events stated in the conclusion happened'. Equally, we must think about the way in which our knowledge of other events and ideas might help us to see the relevance of one particular claim in establishing another and thus prevent us from 'missing' an important relevant premise.

Presenting relevant premises is also about making it *clear* that they are relevant. In other words, use a claim, as part of a linked chain of premises, to show the relevance of the premises to the conclusion. An effective argument or explanation not only reflects careful thinking, but also clearly demonstrates it, so others can follow your reasoning. Here is an example of how to establish relevance:

1. Australia's universities are of a high quality.
2. Australian university graduates report that their lecturers are, generally speaking, good at communicating.
3. All universities now have quality-assurance programs to maintain quality.
4. Australia's universities attract many overseas students to them.

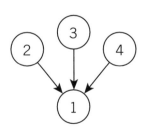

Claim 3 mentions the words 'university' and 'quality' and is demonstrably relevant through this word-similarity with claim 1. Claim 2, while possibly relevant (it certainly mentions some evidence—good communication by university teachers—that we might assume to be relevant), depends on exactly what the conclusion is trying to say. Claim 1, the conclusion, is not well formed. It is vague since it does not make clear whether it is claiming that all aspects of universities are of a high quality or whether (as hinted at by the premises) it is merely the teaching function of universities that is of a high quality (leaving aside, for example, research work).

So the first mistake here is that the conclusion's vagueness makes it unclear whether the premises are relevant. Claim 4 exhibits another problem with relevance. It may, for example, be that overseas students come to Australia because studying here is cheap, or because they like the climate in Australia. Claim 4 becomes a relevant premise only if the reason for the students' preference for Australia is based on the quality of the universities. So the second mistake is that *another* premise ought to have been added to make clear how claim 4 is relevant to claim 1. We might say that, while claim 3 is self-evidently relevant (it provides, in the word 'quality', its own evidence of how it bears on the conclusion), claim 4 is not self-evidently relevant and therefore needs an additional, dependent premise to provide this evidence.

Exercise 6.3

For each of the following claims, write three claims that, in your view, are relevant to showing either why they are true or why they are false (depending on whether you agree with the claims or not).

a. Voting at elections should be compulsory.
b. Protecting the environment is more important than economic development.
c. Australia's unique cultural identity is being overwhelmed by imported American culture.
d. Everyone should own a personal computer.

The special role of framing premises

A framing premise, discussed in chapter 4, is one that in many cases functions to make other premises (in the same chain) relevant to a conclusion—to provide the extra information that, when combined with other claims, shows how they relate to the conclusion. Let us look again at the argument about quality universities. The relevance of claim 4 to claim 1 was not clear. However, if we added another claim to it, 'Overseas students generally seek to study at high-quality universities' (claim 5), then the relevance to claim 1 of this specific piece of evidence would be clearer. We should remember that claims initially connect two component parts. In this case, claim 1 connects universities and quality; claim 4, on the surface, relates universities with another issue—overseas students. This problem can be overcome only if the third claim, claim 5, links together overseas students with quality.

Exercise 6.4

Go back to exercise 6.3 and review what you have done. You will need some further premises to show why the ones you have given are relevant to the four conclusions. Add a premise in each case.

Another example of using an additional claim to show the relevance of one claim to another concerns the use of authority to give a good foundation for claims. In the previous chapter, we saw how a claim can be well founded if it is supported by reference to a relevant authority. Obviously, then, effective reasoning will depend on our judgments of the relevance of various authorities to the claims that we wish to make. But, as before, we must be prepared to demonstrate this relevance. The following is an example we have already considered, but it has been expanded so that our reasoning is transparent:

1. Australian history is marked by considerable conflict and tension over the competing interests of labour and capital.
2. Rickard, Australia: *A Cultural History* (1992) asserts claim 1.
3. Rickard is a relevant authority on such matters.
4. Rickard is a widely published and well-respected Australian historian.
5. If historians are widely published and well respected, then we can be confident that they are a relevant authority.

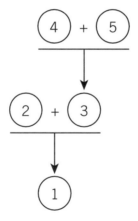

Think about this example and how similar it is to the basic form of reasoning discussed in chapter 3. Can you see that claims 4 and 5 serve to establish that Rickard is indeed a relevant authority, as asserted in claim 3 (and hence go above this claim in the diagram)? Claim 3, in turn, is added to claim 2 (the reference to Rickard's book) to show its relevance in founding claim 1.

From this example we can see that the reasoning that, logically, underpins the simple use of a reference can be long-winded. However, the lesson to learn from this *is not* that we should be so explicit and lengthy in our own work. Rather, when we want to develop an effective argument or explanation, we have to *decide* which premises need to have their relevance substantiated and which premises do not. Making this decision requires that we understand what is expected of us in reasoning. We must also consider the degree to which our audience will accept that what we claim to be relevant really is, even though we give no evidence for its relevance.

Decisions about what to include or not include to establish relevance can only be made by thinking about the context. Imagine if I were to argue that 'all Australians should give due recognition to Aboriginal native title claims' (claim 1) and I gave, broadly, three reasons to show why:

2. Both common law and legislation demand such recognition.
3. Aborigines were the first inhabitants of the continent we now call Australia.
4. Henry Reynolds has written an excellent book on the history of Aboriginal–European relations called *The Other Side of the Frontier* (1980).

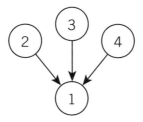

For claim 2, I would not consider it necessary to explain the relevance of the legal position; I would simply assume that my audience would see that a legal requirement was relevant to what all Australians should do. For claim 3, I would consider it necessary to explain to some audiences (perhaps those ignorant of such matters) the relevance of the claim (by adding the claim 'The first inhabitants of a land mass have inalienable rights to that land', claim 5); I would assume that other audiences would see the relevance. For claim 4, I would always seek to explain the relevance of this unusual premise (by adding the claims 'This book incontrovertibly demonstrates the need for reconciliation' and 'native title claims are essential to reconciliation', claim 6).

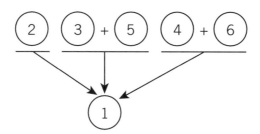

Here is another example that shows how context involves both people and ideas. Students at university usually write for a knowledgeable academic and fail to work carefully through all the issues, assuming that the academic will 'fill in the gaps'. In doing so, they forget that they must also meet one of the contextual requirements of scholarly work: that they *not* make too many assumptions, *not* presume that the audience is clever and will 'get' the point of the essay. Hence many essays fail to achieve the required standard because their authors have not consciously considered and learnt about the context into which they fit. This point is significant in all communication. Whenever we communicate we must actively imagine and reflect on our context and how that might influence the way we present our arguments and explanations.

Exercise 6.5

For the following argument, add claims that satisfactorily show why the given premises (claims 2, 3, and 4) are relevant to the conclusion. Then indicate two contexts for each: one in which you would explicitly establish relevance and one in which you would not.

1. All Australians should learn about their own nation's history.
2. History helps us to understand what is happening now.
3. Australia's history tells many stories of the fight for democracy and justice.
4. Learning about Australian history involves learning to write essays.

Strength of support

It is very important to think about the strength of the support that we can give our claims. There are two distinct issues involved. First of all, we must have good evidence. A well-founded claim, by virtue of the fact that it is well founded, will have a number of good premises, which should be provided to assist our audience in accepting and understanding it. But a more significant issue in communicating our reasoning is to decide which of the supporting claims that we know about should be explicitly stated in our argument or explanation. We should also be able to decide when we need to do more research to find out if the claims we want to make can be supported. The issue of well-founded claims must, in part, depend on an analysis of whether or not the claims are true or not, but it also requires that we consider carefully how we communicate our arguments and explanations. The following discussion addresses this second consideration.

The burden of proof

Even if all the premises are acceptable, and even if they are relevant, you neverthe-less still may not be effective in your reasoning. Why? Because, at base, you must always offer enough support for your audience to be convinced that the conclusion of your argument is acceptable or that the explanation of it is complete. Strength of support is, like relevance, very dependent upon the context in which we are reasoning, and we can never be certain that we have given enough support for our conclusions. On the other hand, if we do think about this context, then we can greatly improve the chances that we will be effective.

The first such context issue concerns the burden of proof. The following example is drawn from a legal situation. In a court case, the two opposing parties do not come to court each with an equal task. In a criminal trial, for example, the prosecution has the burden of proof. If it fails to establish the guilt of the defendant, then the defendant goes free; the defence does not have to prove innocence, but must merely defeat the prosecution's attempts to prove guilt. There are two common measures of the burden of proof in the law. In criminal cases, the prosecution must prove *beyond reasonable doubt* that the defendant is guilty. In civil cases, a less onerous burden is carried by the plaintiff (the one who initiates the action). The plaintiff must prove, *on the balance of probabilities*, that they are right; the respondent's task is to establish a greater probability that their side of the argument is correct.

It is rare, outside legal and quasi-legal contexts, for the burden of proof on one side of an argument to be recognised formally. Yet, the implicit idea behind it is found in all reasoning. One person has a more demanding job of proving a point and, if they fail, then an alternative position remains the preferred one. One person must provide more evidence, must positively show their conclusion to be true. Usually existing conclusions require less evidence or, perhaps, will be taken to be true unless clearly shown otherwise. Obviously, those who have the burden of proof in an argumentative situation will need stronger, more compelling support for their conclusion than their opponents. The problem, however, is to determine where this burden lies.

As with all these contextually based judgments, it is impossible to provide some ready formula by which we can always ascertain the burden of proof—who has it and how onerous it is. Each situation will be different. However, as a general rule, we must (when arguing or explaining) consider the established true claims that conflict with our proposed reasoning. For example:

Historians in twentieth-century Australia had, up until the 1970s, a well-established position on Aboriginal responses to white invasion: Aboriginal people, it was claimed and accepted, did little to resist the encroachment of Europeans' settlement. Both experts and the community agreed; this view was found in numerous books and articles. In fact, few historians even bothered to explore the issue, since they were sure they had the correct answer to the question 'What was the Aborigines' response?'. Then, from about 1972 onwards, historians began to look again at the evidence and come to startling new conclusions. But, as Henry Reynolds, a leading exponent of this historical revision, has noted, he and like-minded historians had to amass significant amounts of compelling evidence before the orthodox view was overturned. Equally, recent arguments that run counter to the new orthodoxy that Aboriginal people resisted in numerous ways have failed—by and large—to achieve much currency, precisely because they do not have enough evidence behind them.[2]

Who is correct is not the issue here. What matters is that we recognise that context creates a background of accepted conclusions and explanations, which if an established position is challenged, *must* be taken into account to decide if the new reasoning provides sufficient support for its conclusions.

Justifying all aspects of the conclusion

As we know, claims are complex statements that tie together all sorts of information about ideas, scope, certainty, values, and so on. As a result, any reasoning to support or explain a claim (the conclusion) must attend to each aspect of that claim. For example, if we wanted to explain why 'Most people do not understand that late capitalism will never sustain unemployment levels lower than 5 per cent', then there are many aspects of the claim that need explanation. At the very least, our premises would need to answer the following questions:

- Why 'Most people' (and not some or all or none)?
- Why do they not understand this point?
- What is late capitalism?
- Why will late capitalism not sustain low unemployment?
- Why 'lower than 5 per cent' (and not a smaller or larger proportion)?
- What is unemployment (does it include, for example, partial employment)?
- Why is the word 'sustain' used?

Part of the trick in reasoning effectively is to frame our conclusions in such a way that we *can* justify all of what they state explicitly. There is no point, for example, in concluding that 'capitalism has never caused social problems'. Even if we wish to argue that capitalism is better than any other economic system, it is better to assert the conclusion in a way that does acknowledge its problems, while still making an argument that it has some advantages. On the other hand, we should not be afraid to state our conclusions (if we believe in them) and then go to the effort of covering all the many aspects involved. For example, the Australian historians, such as Reynolds, who dramatically improved our understanding of Aboriginal–European relations did not back away from their conclusion that Aboriginal people actively and persistently resisted European invasion simply because it was hard to prove. They did the detailed research necessary to establish this conclusion.

Justifying all aspects of the conclusion is particularly necessary when the conclusion contains some value component. The premises must provide support both for the descriptive basis of the claim and for the value judgment that it makes either implicitly or explicitly. For example, to support the conclusion that 'The problem of unemployment in a late capitalist economy demands government regulation of the labour market' carries with it a similar range of issues as the last example. Yet it also concerns further issues regarding the values implicit in the claim. Is unemployment necessarily a problem? It would not be implausible to imagine that some people would favour higher unemployment (as, for example, a way of keeping wage costs down). The trick is to be aware of the connotations of our conclusions—those less obvious meanings and implications, which even though they are not explicit in the stated claim, nevertheless require explanation or argument. Such an awareness is the hallmark of effective reasoning. Once again, it is the context (audience, general expectations, and so on) that makes clear what connotations we might need to consider. Arguments about Aboriginal–European relations, for example, now occur in a context that is completely different to that of thirty years ago, precisely because general knowledge among Australians about this issue has changed and the attitudes towards Aboriginal people among white Australians are somewhat more positive than in the 1970s.

Breadth of premises

It is rare to find a claim that is so simple in what it asserts about the world that it can be easily supported by one or two premises; what is more, when explaining why an event has occurred, the reasons on which our explanation are based are likely to be highly complex. Hence, as well as giving depth to each individual reason (expressed as a chain of premises), we also need to give a broad argument when required. Such breadth ensures that reasoning is not rendered ineffective by oversimplification. There is, of course, no general rule regarding how much information should be given in support of a conclusion: it depends on the conclusion and the context. No reason should be given that is irrelevant to the conclusion. Yet we should not exclude *relevant* information; otherwise we will not deal with the full complexity of an issue.

The need for breadth is particularly evident in reasoning about why things have happened or why they might in future happen (cause and effect). For example, if we were to argue that 'Australia's current rate of immigration is too low', we could develop a series of arguments about the effects of low immigration, drawing on various aspects of this topic. Without at the moment unpacking them into complete premises, there are at least four different 'reasons':

a   A larger population provides significant economic benefits.
b   Higher immigration provides significant cultural benefits.
c   Higher immigration is a sign to the rest of the world that Australia is a good international citizen.
d   Higher immigration will increase Australia's defence capabilities.

Each reason concerns a different aspect of the problem—a different point that, independently, supports the conclusion. Why would a collection of reasons be needed here? Well, to say simply that the economy benefits may be countered by an argument that there is no point in having a strong economy if the result is an impoverished culture. In such a situation, the conclusion may well not be accepted and our argument would be ineffective. Or, for example, if we were to fail to provide reason **c**, those people in our audience who would themselves argue for the primacy of international relations in determining economic, cultural, and defence conditions might not be convinced.

As we might expect, for most claims there are arguments for and against; there are explanations from one angle and another. Whenever we reason, we are, by definition, setting up an opposition with possible counter-arguments. To give sufficient support to our own conclusion, we must give evidence that defeats, or at least casts doubt on, likely counter-arguments in advance of them actually being mounted against what we are proposing. For example, we know that one significant reason that opposes our conclusion that 'Australia's current rate of immigration is too low' is that 'social tensions will increase with increased immigration'. If we know in advance that such a counter-reason exists and we fail to address it, then we are making our reasoning less effective. First, we run the risk of appearing to have failed to understand all the relevant issues (and thus casting doubt on our overall competence). Second, we may find people unconvinced of our conclusion, even though they accept all of the positive reasons we give. The response of such people might be: 'Well, defence, politics, culture, and the economy will all improve, but that means nothing if the society that all those other things serve is falling apart'. That we disagree will not matter; the error we will have made is that our disagreement has not been included in the original argument we presented. So, in general terms, effective reasoning requires that we cover all the relevant issues involved in establishing or explaining our conclusion, whether they are positive or negative.[3]

We do need to consider whether or not our arguments and explanations meet objective criteria of strength. We need to consider whether they are well founded and strong *regardless* of what any particular audience thinks of them. However, because knowledge is never used or useful outside a social, non-objective context,[4] we must also consider the audiences of our reasoning. Hence breadth of premises can best be understood in relation to the burden of proof. In essence, to meet our burden of proof, we must mainly meet the expectations of our audiences, but not simply 'give in' to what they want to hear.

If an audience, for example, expects to see, in a discussion of contemporary European–Aboriginal relations, some consideration of the history of those relations, then we would be failing our audience if we did not offer it or did not, at least, dismiss the relevance of such a consideration. Which approach we would use, of course, depends on our views of the topic, but as a general rule, it is fair to say that our arguments must address (either positively or negatively) those aspects of a topic that we guess our audience is expecting to see covered in our reasoning. Furthermore, if the members of our audience have mixed backgrounds—with some being more convinced by and interested in economic arguments, others by historical arguments, and a third group by purely moral or ethical arguments—then all groups would need to be covered. By contrast, in a report on the legal aspects of European–Aboriginal relations, the audience's expectations would be narrower: the context of the report ('legal aspects') would exclude other reasons, which if we were to introduce them, might actually weaken our arguments because they would be irrelevant to the particular issue being reported on.

In summary, not only do we need to understand issues well, but we must also understand our audience and other contextual factors so that we can judge what should or should not be included in any argument or explanation.

Exercise 6.6

Take any argument or explanation that you are writing at the moment or have recently written. Begin by establishing clearly in your own mind the context for your work, including its audience, and the sorts of constraints or requirements that the context places on you. Step by step, apply to it all of the issues discussed in this section, with the aim of improving it.

Coherence in scope and certainty

Finally, we must consider the relationship between what we are claiming as our conclusion and the evidence used to support it, as expressed through the scope and certainty aspects of the claims. If the premises and conclusion are coherent in this respect, then our reasoning is more effective. Coherence of scope, while always important, is particularly significant in reasoning from specific cases. Here is an example:

> John has met a few Aborigines who are alcoholics, and therefore he concludes that all Aboriginal people are alcoholics.

The error John makes here is that the scope of his premise ('a few') is not coherent with the scope of the conclusion ('all'). Hence he has overgeneralised in his conclusion. Similarly, if John was to visit one Aboriginal community in which, say, a third of its members were alcoholics, he would also be wrong to conclude that 'A third of all Aboriginal people are alcoholics'. The scope of his premises (just one community) is not coherent with the conclusion about *all* Aborigines, since that community is most unlikely to be a representative sample of the entire Aboriginal population. However, if John were to continue his investigations and discover that, say, 70 per cent of Aboriginal people in outback areas suffer from poor health, he would be equally in error to conclude that 'Poor health is, thus, a small problem for outback Aboriginals'. Such a conclusion understates the extent of the situation and again reflects a lack of coherence between premise and conclusion. General conclusions are not, of themselves, the problem: we could not think and know without reasonable generalisations. Rather, we must always be sure that the generalisations are properly grounded in the specific cases on which they rely.

Issues of scope and certainty are also important in *reasoning from generalisation*. The purpose of linking together a particular case with a general rule in the premises is to then draw a conclusion about that specific case based on the generalisation. The scope of the conclusion, therefore, must be coherent with the generalisation. The following example shows good coherence:

> The incidence of major earthquakes in areas located away from major tectonic fault-lines is low; Australia is such an area, and hence we can predict that Australia will rarely suffer from major earthquakes.

However, another example demonstrates poor coherence:

> Generally speaking, students at Australian universities receive a high-quality education. Ho Ming intends to study at the University of Melbourne and fears that he will not receive a high-quality education.

On the basis of the premise, Ho is wrong to hold these fears.

Exercise 6.7

Look at the following conclusions. Without thinking about whether they are true, and thinking only about the words as they appear in front of you (especially those that define the scope and certainty of the conclusion), indicate which conclusions are milder and which are stronger (in relation to one another). Then think about the sorts of audiences that would need more or less argument to persuade them. Who would easily be persuaded of the conclusions? Who would be sceptical of these conclusions?

    a. All Australians should be forced to do national military service.
    b. One option is to consider limited military service for some young Australians.
    c. We should definitely establish an inquiry to consider the possibility of introducing national military service.

Review

Effective reasoning requires that we attend to a wide variety of factors, both in our analysis of the connections between claims and then in the presentation of those claims and connections. We cannot, truly, separate out the needs of effective analysis and presentation, since our analysis will always be influenced by the context in which reasoning occurs, and that context is, by and large, determined by the knowledge and expectations of our likely audience.

Some of the ways to be more effective in reasoning concern the links between premises: if we make these links well, unpacking any initial 'reason' for a conclusion into a clear chain of dependent premises, then our analysis has depth. In particular, we must avoid allowing any claims that are doubtful to remain implicit, or failing to make explicit links between claims that are not obvious; such assumptions can only be tested if we are explicit about all the necessary claims in the chain. Equally, we must not confuse claims that support another claim (diagrammed above the claim being supported) with claims that are dependent (diagrammed alongside one another).

The relationships of premises above with conclusion below are only strong if the premises are relevant and provide strong support. We judge relevance by looking at whether or not the premise is connected in some way to the conclusion (through the form of words or the issues involved or via some background knowledge). To establish relevance, we can include a framing premise if necessary or write our claims more carefully. Premises provide sufficient support for a conclusion if, in context, other people will judge the degree of support to be sufficient. We can ensure effective reasoning only by making sure that we satisfy any burden of proof we have, attending to the detail of our conclusion (justifying all aspects of it), making sure there is coherence between scope and certainty, and reasoning broadly where necessary.

CONCEPT CHECK

The following terms and concepts are introduced in this chapter. Before checking in the Glossary, write a short definition of each term:

breadth of reasoning

burden of proof

depth of reasoning

relevance

strength of support

Review exercise 6

Answer briefly the following questions, giving, where possible, an example in your answer that is different from those used in this book:

a. How many reasons does a chain of dependent premises offer in support of a conclusion?
b. What is an implied premise?
c. What is the difference between the relevance and acceptability of a claim?
d. How might a framing premise be used in connection with relevance?
e. What role does the idea of well-founded claims play in relation to relevance and support?
f. What is the difference between depth and breadth of reasoning?
g. How can we use scope and certainty to judge the effectiveness of reasoning?

h. What role does context (and especially audience) play in effective reasoning?

NOTES

1   In the process of unpacking, however, we usually think of additional, separate reasons that did not immediately occur to us. For example, in thinking through the detail of the economic reason, we might also come up with other reasons. One that occurs to me is that there is a moral argument concerning the rights of citizens to free education.

2   See the introduction to H. Reynolds, *The Other Side of the Frontier*, Penguin Books, Melbourne, 1980.

3   Note that this requirement to think ahead about counter-arguments is particularly important in written reasoning. In a conversation, we have an immediate opportunity to respond to objections, but in a written argument, there are no such opportunities.

4   See chapter 9 for a brief discussion of objective strength (determined without reference to audience) as opposed to intersubjective strength (in which the audience plays a significant role). This complex philosophical debate is too involved to discuss here and, whether or not you believe that knowledge can be objectively true, the need to think about audiences remains very important.

7

What Kinds of Reasoning are There?

We have now finished with our detailed look at the analytical structure approach. This chapter will consider, in a more general way, how to think about the types of reasoning we might use and encounter. I already noted, in chapter 2, that basically reasoning is either about relationships across time (cause and effect), or within the sets or groups into which we divide and classify objects at any given moment. But there are some other ways of thinking about reasoning that are worth exploring in more detail, while recognising that there is no set way to classify or assert that you are using 'one type of reasoning' but not another. In this chapter we will:

1 Examine the difference between deductive and inductive reasoning—a commonly misunderstood difference.

2 Look at the difference between categorical and propositional logic, to discover in particular how propositions ('if..., then...') can be useful.

3 Look at five types of reasoning, known as reasoning from cause, generalisation, specific cases, analogy, and terms (i.e. definitional).

Deductive and inductive reasoning

A common error

The difference between deduction and induction is one of the more vexed issues in contemporary logic. Exactly how (and why) we distinguish between them is subject both to erroneous views and legitimate disagreements. First, let me dispose of a common error, one that has probably been taught to you (or you have read) at some stage. It is often claimed that deduction is a form of reasoning from general rules to specific premises and that induction is the reverse, that is, reasoning from specific cases to a general conclusion. Now, no matter what you might see or read elsewhere, this is wrong. The difference between deduction and induction has nothing to do with general or specific reasoning, but has everything to do with what the conclusion does on the basis of the premises.

We will explore this genuine difference in a moment but let me reassure you that, if the distinction seems hard to grasp, you are not alone. Philosophers have generally sought to retreat to those examples and cases of reasoning which are clearly deductive and clearly inductive: they have not engaged with the muddy mass of indistinct cases which are, by and large, the everyday reasoning we use.

Deduction

In deductive reasoning, your conclusion states with certainty a relationship between two or more premises. It has to be certain, because it simply makes explicit a relationship that is already there (but not directly obvious) in the combination of the claims that are serving as premises. You will remember this aspect from the discussion of claims in chapters 2 to 4. Let us look at an example:

I am under 18; people under 18 in Australia cannot vote. Therefore I cannot vote.

There are three key terms in this argument. One is age (under 18); the other is voting; and the last is 'I'. The conclusion simply re-expresses the implicit relationship of the premises which can be expressed, in a formula way, like this:

A is one of B; B can't do C; therefore A can't do C.

The certainty with which (in this argument) the conclusion is stated relates not to the truth or otherwise of the premises but to the logical form of the argument. If it turns out that the premises are indeed true, then the conclusion is guaranteed both by the truth of the premises and by the form of the reasoning.

The key test for a deductive argument is to ask yourself, being absolutely trusting, 'can you deny the conclusion, if it is that you previously have no doubt or deny the premises'. For example:

African swallows are migratory birds; all migratory birds fly long distances and therefore I conclude African swallows fly long distances.

Now, let us assume absolutely and without doubt that the premises are true. Can you deny (refuse to accept) the conclusion now? No! Do not be confused and think 'Ah, but maybe African swallows are not migratory birds'; if you have this doubt then you have not accepted the first premise. Deductive thinking is something of a mind game (an important one, nevertheless): checking for deductive entailment (where the conclusion is guaranteed by the premises) first of all proceeds from the assumption that the premises are absolutely correct. If they are, then you simply need to check that the conclusion follows logically from them. Only then can you go back and see if there are doubts about the premises.

Induction

In an inductive argument, unlike deduction, if the premises are true, then the conclusion is only probably true and how big a chance that it is true depends on the weight of evidence presented in the premises. The conclusion, then, in an inductive argument is not guaranteed by the premises, but only supported by them. Often, the difference expresses itself in the way that an inductive conclusion does not state an implicit relationship but goes beyond the premises to make a new claim altogether. Here is an example:

> Imagine that, in the best traditions of the board game *Cluedo*, you are conducting a murder investigation. Mr Green's body has been found stabbed to death. In the course of your investigations, you discover that:
>
> > Mr White says he saw Mr Black stab Green.
> > Black is well known to have hated Green.
> > Green's blood is found on Black's hands.
> > Ms Yellow heard Green gasp 'Black is stabbing me!'

These four claims serve as reasonably compelling evidence that Mr Black was the murderer. However, can you be certain? No. You can only gather evidence to increase the probability that you are correct in judging Black to be the murderer. Indeed, if this case were to go to court, then the test used by the jury to convict or not convict would be one of 'reasonable doubt'. The jury would not have to be 100 per cent certain, simply convinced beyond a reasonable doubt that Black was guilty. So, although you would accuse Black as if you were certain he was the murderer, in purely logical terms you would not have deduced that conclusion from the evidence, but have induced it and thus always be fractionally short of absolute certainty. Remember that the claim which serves as the conclusion in this argument 'Black killed Green' is not completely implied in the premises, as we shall see ...

> You, being a good detective, do some more checking and discover that:
>
> > White told people Black hated Green.
> > Black got bloody trying to help Green.
> > White disguised himself as Black to do the job.

Hence, the probability now swings around to White being the murderer. Again, you cannot be certain, but would probably now proceed to accuse White. Induction, then, is the process of gathering evidence and, rather than stating something already completely contained in the premises (but not openly stated), making some prediction or estimate of what the most likely conclusion would be given that evidence.

The lesson to learn here is: if you think about the kinds of complex arguments that you have been developing in earlier chapters of this book, what you will probably see is that, towards the end of a complex argument, the reasoning will become deductive, carefully delineating a logical set of relationships that, in the earlier parts of the complex argument have been established through inductive reasoning.

Categorical and propositional logic

Now we will look at the two common forms of deductive reasoning. For a long time, logic was primarily thought to consist in the formation of definitive relationships (such as the deductive examples above), normally expressed in the form:

Humans are mammals.
All mammals breathe air.
Therefore humans breathe air.

Such reasoning is called categorical precisely because it is not about actual events so much as the ideal categories by which we can define and discriminate the innumerable things in the world into a regular pattern or order. What is significant is that categorical logic is mostly associated with European thinking *prior* to the modern era of scientific investigation and the constant quest to discover what was new, rather than earlier attempts to precisely define a never-changing pattern of categories and attributes. It should also be noted that this form of reasoning depends absolutely on how we define terms such as air and breathe, and how precisely we use words in our claims. Technically fish also breathe—they breathe water and extract from it, if not 'air' then air's constituent elements. Yet fish are not mammals. Thus while useful to understand, categorical reasoning is more interesting for our purposes in that it models how dominant forms of reasoning are bound up in the social order of their time.

Propositional logic on the other hand depends upon propositions: statements that propose a relationship between two states of affairs. Technically these statements should be expressed as 'if..., then...' claims. However it is possible to write them in such a way as to imply, rather than explicitly state, the propositional nature of the claim. If the Ancient Greeks spent a lot of time philosophising about how specific items and general groups might be put together and thus developed categorical logic to a fine art, in the nineteenth century, European philosophers became fascinated by propositional logic. If/then statements are, probably, at the heart of most of our reasoning, even though we often do not realise it. They link together one event (the 'if' part) and propose that if it happens, then something else will also occur. It is, perhaps, the philosopher's version of Newton's third law of thermodynamics, which stated that all actions have an opposite and equal reaction. Let us have a look at an example which uses a series of if/then statements to prove that Australia's economic health depends, not on low wages, but on high wages:

1. If Australia's wages are reduced, then people will have less to spend.
2. If people have less to spend, then consumption will fall.
3. If consumption falls, then the economy will slow down.
4. If the economy slows, then business profits will fall.
5. Therefore, if we want to avoid a loss in profit, we must not reduce wages.

The power and flexibility of propositional logic is demonstrated by this example, not because these premises guarantee the conclusion is true, but rather because they create a series of logical relationships between two otherwise apparently unconnected events—the need to avoid a loss in profit and the desire not to reduce wages. If we were then to set about convincing someone of this ultimate conclusion, we would, by having set up the chain of propositions in this manner, have identified the key sub-conclusions that would each need to be supported by sub-arguments. Thus, we would have to establish that it was indeed reasonable to believe that 'If consumption falls, then the economy will slow down', and we might do this by reference to real-world examples such as previous economic conditions in which a fall in consumption has indeed caused an economic slowdown.

The lesson to learn here is: while categorical logic concerns itself with the structural relationship of the categories we use, defining the inclusions and exclusions so that we can be sure what does or does not belong together as a group, propositional logic prompts us to ask the right questions about what we need to establish, inductively, to then make our overall argument convincing.

Five types of reasoning

It is important to recognise that these five types are not mutually exclusive. We will consider causal reasoning but, for example, we also see that when looking at causes we are also asserting analogies between the cause of one event and another. Equally, when we look at analogies, there are ways in which analogical reasoning is the same as reasoning from generalisations or might involve causal relationships. Thus, the five types presented here are not done so in the same manner as the discussion of deduction/induction which showed how arguments of one type (in each case) could not be of the other type. Rather, I present these five types to assist you in thinking more broadly about the kinds of questions you might ask in your reasoning and (as we will see in chapter 8) to guide your search for information.

Causal reasoning

Reasoning from cause is very common and we are all familiar with it, if only in a common-sense way. If someone asks you 'Why did you buy this book?', you might reply 'because it was reasonably cheap and looked interesting'; alternatively you might say 'because someone recommended that I buy it' or even 'because it was a compulsory textbook for my studies'. In all cases, you have stated what event or fact caused you to buy this book. Hence, in a causal relationship between claims, the premise or premises state the *cause*, and the conclusion states the *effect* resulting from that cause.

Now, very often we use a simple causal *claim*, such as 'Australia's economic weakness in the world economy is caused by its reliance on commodity exports'. As we know, a claim does have an internal connection between the cause and the effect. We should be careful to remember that a single claim, such as the one just given, is not an argument or explanation. However, this claim does imply that it is the result of (or conclusion to) causal reasoning. So, in making good links between premises and conclusions, where we are reasoning about cause and effect, we need to spell out what that relationship is. For example:

> Australia is reliant on commodity exports; such exports are always at risk of natural disasters and price fluctuations; these risks lead to weakness, and hence, Australia has a weak economy in global terms.

When we are attempting to link claims in order to express a causal relationship, there are two general rules that are particularly useful. First of all, we can look for the factor that is the only *difference* between two given situations. For example:

> Before recent changes to industrial relations laws, labour unions could not be excluded by employers from most wage negotiations; now they can be. Not much else has changed, however. Since this legislative change took place, average wages have declined dramatically. Hence, I conclude that the likely cause of this reduction in wages has been the exclusion of unions from wage negotiations.

The two situations that are being compared are the higher level of average wages in the past and the lower level of average wages now. The argument in the example seeks to establish that the only differing factor in these two situations, which might explain the change in wage levels, is the exclusion of unions. We can express this rule thus:

> X is the cause of Y because the only relevant difference between Y happening and not happening is that X was only present when Y happened.

The second general rule for determining causal relationships requires us to look for the only *similarity* or common element in two or more situations. Take the following argument as an example:

Jones and Wilson have both been sacked by the company that used to employ them. Jones, a middle-aged male cleaner, was a poor worker with a history of arriving late; Wilson, a young woman working as a filing clerk, had always been judged by her boss to be a competent worker. But both Jones and Wilson had just been elected union delegates, and thus, I would reasonably conclude that it was their active participation in the union that led to their dismissal.

The differences between the two workers contrast with their similar treatment (both were sacked); so, the only other similarity between them (that they were union delegates) seems to be the likely cause of their dismissal. We can express this rule thus:

X is the cause of Y because it is the only relevant similarity between two separate occurrences of Y happening.

The other key aspect to causal reasoning is to appreciate that some causal events are necessary, and others are sufficient. If I assert that oxygen is necessary for a fire to occur, I am not saying that oxygen causes fires. Thus the presence of oxygen is a necessary condition, but not sufficient. However, while a lighted match is sufficient to set fire to a pile of dry paper if dropped on it, it is not necessary — I could also use a flamethrower or focus the heat of the sun with a magnifying glass.

In the many complex causal situations that we encounter, it will be impossible to isolate the only relevant difference or the only relevant similarity. We will also struggle to determine necessary and sufficient causes because we cannot (normally) conduct repeated experiments in which we determine the relative state of each causal element. Rather, we will normally be confronted by a whole jumble of possible differences and similarities. So, the main function of our investigation of causes, and of the resulting causal arguments and explanations we write, will be to assign some significance to each cause (was it a minor or major cause? was it significant enough to count as a sufficient cause on its own?) or to discover the interrelationship between causes. We also need to consider the degree to which each cause was beyond or within human control (was the cause a direct human action, or something in the general environment?). Further, we need to avoid assuming, simply because events happen in close proximity to one another, that they are necessarily related as cause and effect. Perhaps it was simply a coincidence that, for example, the two workers were sacked. Alternatively, we might argue, in relation to the first example, that there is a common cause: wage reductions and union exclusion are not necessarily effect and cause but, rather, could both be the effects of some other cause—perhaps structural changes in the political economy of Australia.

Reasoning from generalisation

Reasoning from generalisation is another common form of argument or explanation. Yet it is very different from causation. If causation, at its simplest, seeks to show how one event leads to another, reasoning from generalisation shows how knowledge about a general class or category of events allows us to make a conclusion about a specific event that fits the general category. For example:

All children who have been fully immunised are protected against some common and life-threatening diseases, such as whooping cough, polio, and diphtheria. Therefore, Steven, who has been immunised, is most unlikely to fall sick with these diseases.

The general form of such arguments is as follows:

Class X is defined by the fact that the individual cases within that class all have property A in common; hence any individual case that is a member of that class will also exhibit property A.

So, arguing from a generalisation involves two distinct steps. First of all, it must be established that the specific case does indeed fit the general class that is proposed, that it is *consistent*. Once that 'fit' is established, then we must draw a conclusion that relies, not on our knowledge of the specific case, but our knowledge of the general class.

Imagine, for a moment, that you are a doctor. A woman comes to see you with the following symptoms: swollen glands, sore throat, weakness in the muscles, and a rash of small red spots across the back and chest. You are not sure what is wrong with the patient but can use reasoning to make a diagnosis: 'Almost all people who have these symptoms are suffering from measles; this particular patient has these symptoms; therefore she is suffering from measles'. Further, you can determine treatment on the basis of the generalisation that 'All people suffering from the measles need to spend a week resting in bed and take antibiotics to prevent secondary infections'. You know, with reasonable confidence, that this patient has measles and so can prescribe this treatment for her.

Let us explore this form of relationship by imagining that a class is like a box into which we put all the items that are the same as one another. On the lid of this box are a list of requirements that determine which items can and cannot be included. Patients who have the swollen glands and sore throat, but not the red spots, could not be placed in the 'measles sufferer' class because they would not meet all the requirements. Patients with the red spots but no other symptoms would also fail to qualify (they probably have a skin irritation instead). However, as well as a set of requirements for membership of a class or category, a generalisation also includes a judgment that sums up the nature of those items in the category ('people with these symptoms have measles'). Hence there are two aspects to a generalisation: a condition that determines what specific cases fit into the generalisation, and another condition that states the common consequence or state relating to that generalisation.

When we are confident about our generalisations, and a specific case does fit a particular general category, then reasoning from generalisations is very easy and effective. The trick is in making that initial judgment about the relationship between the specific case and the generalisation, as expressed in the premises, so that our conclusion (also about the specific case) is well supported. At the same time, we should recognise that many items fit a number of generalisations—that often an 'item' has many conflicting qualities or components that make it hard to judge the appropriate generalisation. For example, doctors are often confronted with a series of symptoms in a patient that could mean any one of a number of illnesses. The tests that doctors perform are designed to work out exactly which 'generalisation' to apply to the specific patient and thus make sure that the correct treatment is prescribed.

Reasoning from specific cases

Where do these generalisations come from? Do we just make them up? No, in most cases they have been established via reasoning—in this instance, from specific cases to a generalisation. The difference in reasoning from specific cases is that, although a general statement is involved, it is not used as a premise but as the conclusion. We routinely find such reasoning in, for example, opinion polls, statistical analyses, or any other surveys in which the reasoning supports conclusions that generalise beyond the specific scope of those premises. For example, I might argue from specific cases in this manner:

> I have surveyed 1000 Australians, from all social classes and ethnic backgrounds, and 70 per cent of them tell me that they favour changing from a monarchy to a republic. Hence, I would conclude that most Australians also support this change. Ninety per cent of the respondents who were born overseas or whose parents were born overseas were positive about Australia becoming a republic. Hence, I further conclude that republican sentiment will be strongest among the newer members of the Australian community.

There are two conclusions here; each is a general statement about what *all* Australians think, based on a sample of 1000 specific cases. The premises provide a summary of the many specific cases. Nevertheless, relative to the premises, the conclusions are much broader assertions ('most Australians' and 'newer members'). The general form of such arguments is as follows:

> Specific cases (x) of the general category X show the common property A; hence, generally speaking, we can expect all members of the category X to have the common property A.

Reasoning from specific cases depends on the same sorts of judgments about the underlying relationship between the cases and the general category that we encountered in the previous section on reasoning from generalisations. If, for example, I had 'unluckily' chosen a sample of 1000 Australians who were unusually pro-republic, then it is unlikely that my broad conclusions would be correct. So, good reasoning from specific cases requires some consideration of the degree to which the cases selected represent the general category as a whole.

This question of 'representativeness' is precisely why reasoning from specific cases needs to proceed on a sound base of 'specifics'. If I were to argue, on the basis of one bad meal of Italian food, that *all* Italian food was bad, I would be relying on far too small a sample for my argument to be effective. Equally, we should not trust surveys that rely on large numbers of responses from an unrepresentative group. For example, television stations have taken to conducting 'polls' in which people ring in to answer 'yes' or 'no' to a particular question (for example, 'Should the death penalty be reintroduced?'). The answer is then represented as a good generalisation of all Australians' attitudes when, in fact, it is only a generalisation of the views of *those* viewers of *that* particular television station who were *able and willing* to ring in.

Reasoning from analogy

An analogy is a special form of reasoning, which has some similarities with reasoning from specific cases. Reasoning by analogy involves drawing an equally specific conclusion from specific premises via a comparison of like aspects. Good analogies avoid comparisons between items that have too many dissimilarities. For example:

> Imagine a friend gave you a guinea pig to look after but forgot to tell you anything about what to feed it. You might say to yourself, 'I have a guinea pig and do not know what to feed it; but I do know that my rabbit eats carrots, and that rabbits and guinea pigs are similar. Hence, I can probably feed my guinea pig carrots as well'.

Such arguments take the following general form:

> An analogy between X and Y (in the premises) supports a conclusion about Y by showing that the conclusion is true of X; and X and Y are similar in sufficient relevant respects and are not relevantly dissimilar.

You need to be careful to make sure that you are comparing things that are similar in a *relevant* way. Take the following example of reasoning:

> Shaving cream is clearly similar in colour, texture, moistness, and body to whipped cream, and I know that whipped cream is delicious on fruit salad. Hence, shaving cream is delicious on fruit salad.

Do you see what is wrong? The two types of cream are similar, but they are definitely *not* similar in respect of the one main characteristic involved in fruit salad eating: how they *taste*. This question of relevance has been explored in more detail in chapter 6.

While generalised and specific reasoning both depend on classifications of individual cases in relation to general categories, analogies depend on comparison and consistency between equally specific or equally general cases. First of all, good analogies that do not directly involve values are formed through comparing different things on the basis of *consistency of knowledge*. That is, we look around for known cases that are similar to the unknown case, so that we are better able to predict what we will find out. For example, if we knew that large oil spills at sea destroy the salt-water environment, we might also predict that similar spills in a freshwater lake would have a similarly destructive impact. Such analogies depend on the extent to which we are sure that the world is a consistent place, and that it is very unlikely we will find radical differences between cases similar in many respects.

Second, good analogies that involve *values* are formed through comparing different things on the basis of *consistency of action or belief*. That is, we can use known cases that have known types of action or belief associated with them and that are similar to the unknown case to thereby conclude that similar actions or beliefs can be expected in those cases. Such analogies depend on the assumption that the world ought to be a consistent place and, to the extent that we can control what we do in the world, that we should always try to do the same things in similar situations. For example, we would think it most unreasonable if, of three cars parked illegally, only ours was given a parking ticket: such rules need to be applied consistently and we expect that they will be.

Reasoning from terms

The final type of reasoning is less common but equally important. Some claims, as we have seen, establish the definition of a particular word or phrase. Often we need to give reasons for our definitions, either because there is some widespread doubt about them or because we are trying to establish a particular meaning in a given context. Here is an example:

> In a true democracy, all power rests with the people; constitutionally speaking, in a monarchy some power theoretically resides with the monarch. Hence, a monarchy is not democratic.

Now, generally speaking, many monarchies (such as Australia) are democratic; however, this argument establishes that, in a particular context (constitutional theory), monarchies must be defined as undemocratic. While this definition may seem unusual and even irrelevant to daily life in countries such as Australia, it does have some utility within that limited context nevertheless. We tend to find that, by its nature, definitional reasoning is deductive.

Exercise 7.1

Write arguments or explanations using each of the types of reasoning just discussed. You should write these examples in the analytical structure format (that is, as a list of claims and a diagram). Choose issues that are important to you and about which you have some knowledge. You will probably find that each one combines some elements of more than one type.

Review

This chapter has discussed various ways to think about reasoning. You have learnt about the difference between induction and deduction: the most important point to remember from this comparison is that some kinds of reasoning are about the inherent logic of the way we describe the world in words: that there are logical relationships built into claims which, necessarily, lead to other claims. Now this kind of reasoning is not investigative but is the foundation on which inductive reasoning (where you do observe and investigate the world) is based.

You have also learnt about propositional logic which, again, is all about the way you can use a claim that proposes how two other claims are related. Whether or not, in the narrative flow, you actually write a claim in the standard 'if/then' format doesn't matter: very often, when we reason, we are using propositions that, if we rewrote them more accurately, would have to be in that form. Propositional logic is a very important way of finding the links between apparently disparate events and drawing them together into a conclusion.

You have also considered what I call five types of reasoning. These are not 'types' like induction and deduction—an argument may contain elements of (say) reasoning from terms, generalisation, and analogy, all through it. But an argument can only ever be either inductive or deductive. So, these types of reasoning are presented simply to help open your eyes to the ways in which you need to think about your reasoning to make it better.

Thus, what we learn by considering those five types of reasoning is that all argument and explanation starts with a consideration of similarity and difference; commonality and inconsistency; necessity and sufficiency. These concepts are an underlying part of chapters 8 and 9, where we look at how to find information and how to think it through.

CONCEPT CHECK

The following terms and concepts are introduced in this chapter. Before checking in the Glossary, write a short definition of each term:

analogy, reasoning from

cause, reasoning from

consistency

deduction

generalisation, reasoning from

induction

propositional logic

specific cases, reasoning from

terms, reasoning from

Review exercise 7

Answer briefly the following questions, giving, where possible, an example in your answer that is different from those used in this book.

a. What is the difference between deduction and induction?
b. What is the relationship between the idea of internal connections and propositional logic?
c. How can we work out whether one event causes another?
d. What is the purpose of giving a general rule as a premise?
e. What is the 'leap of faith' when we use a selection of cases to assert a more general conclusion?
f. How does an example given as a premise attempt to support its conclusion?
g. How do I determine if an analogy is reasonable?
h. What is the point of using reasoning from terms?

8

Research, Reasoning,
and Analysis

Advice on research usually covers 'physical' issues such as finding books, conducting experiments, and searching computer databases. Such advice does not, however, address the key point that, since knowledge and reasoning are intimately connected, then searching for knowledge is a part of reasoning. The common thread between research and reasoning is that they both involve analysis: the thinking through of the connections between claims (or information). If we cannot consciously control our analysis (our 'thinking moves'), then our research will fail to address the particular needs of the argument or explanation that we develop on the basis of what we discover. Furthermore, there is an easy way to conceptualise what we mean by analysis: it simply involves a constant process of asking questions. Questioning and testing possibilities are the most important 'thinking moves'.

Four aspects of research, reasoning, and analysis will be discussed in this chapter:

1   We will look at knowledge in more detail. Reasoning depends absolutely on knowledge; knowledge is the way that innumerable little pieces of information about the world are linked. Questions are a way of expressing and testing these links and, hence, are the crucial component of analysis.

2   We will then look at four perspectives on the process of finding information (what some might call doing research) as a reasoning process. We will look at:

    • Information understood by where we find it.
    • Information as it relates to other information.
    • Information classified by the topic under investigation.

- Information as it relates to how we are using it.
3 We will examine some general issues to do with sources. Sources can only be used effectively if we understand that the context in which the source was created is different from the context in which we are using the information from that source. If we do not recognise this change in context, we are not properly analysing that information.
4 We will look at how questions can guide our search, and at how we can take information away from our sources, not just as 'information', but in a form that can easily be inserted into our arguments and explanations.

Reasoning and analysis
Reasoning and knowledge

What any one individual knows about the world is extremely limited. People tend to be experts in certain small areas and ignorant in many others; their detailed knowledge is often applicable only in limited situations. It could not be otherwise in modern society, considering the quantities of available information and consequent demands for specialisation. You do not need to be a walking storehouse of information about everything, since there are many places to look if you need to fill in gaps in your knowledge. Moreover, there are many well-established research techniques to generate new data. In such circumstances, the truly knowledgeable people are those who are aware of what they do not know and who have skills in searching. These skills do *not* just involve knowing where and how to look for information (for example, the ability to search the Internet for library holdings of a particular newspaper; technical skill in interviewing; the ability to perform an experiment). Much more importantly, searching skills involve an awareness of how the skills are related to the process of reasoning.

We often think that 'finding things out' precedes 'thinking about them'. In fact, just as writing and speaking (the narrative flow) are bound up with reasoning (analytical structuring), the process of gathering the information also involves many of the important 'thinking moves' that constitute our analysis. If we are unaware of these 'thinking moves', then much of our research will be ineffective or confusing. Reading, interviewing, experimenting, or any of the many research processes are not just about finding out information; they are necessarily processes of analysis.

Reasoning is not the *result* of knowing things: knowledge and reasoning are part and parcel of one another. Knowledge consists of both individual claims *and* the links between them, and hence must be expressed through arguments and explanations. We learn knowledge by understanding these arguments and explanations. Even the most specific statement of what we know (a single claim) requires a connection between more than one idea. What we know is best thought of as a network of interrelated claims—a series of potential, unexpressed arguments and explanations in our heads and in what we read and observe. Hence, knowledge is about relationships: our reasoning compared to, drawn from, contrasted with, and generally taken together with the reasoning of others. One of the best ways to understand how 'finding things out' involves various analytical processes is to consider how questions (which can be used to guide our research) are, in fact, deeply implicated in reasoning.

Reasoned analysis as questions

It is usually thought that the key to scholarly, intellectual work is finding the answers. Well, it is not. Critical academic work about any topic is designed, first and foremost, to discover the right *questions* to ask; the answers come later, once those questions have been determined. While smart thinking is usually more pragmatic than the reflective work done by intellectuals, the same general rule applies in developing our analysis. Thinking *first* about questions is much smarter than trying to think first about answers.

We can understand the significance of questions by thinking about their relationship to the basic process of reasoning—the linking of claims. For example, if I ask 'Does the historical racism of white Australia towards Asians still interfere with Australia's diplomatic relations with Malaysia?', then I am tentatively making the claim 'the historical racism of white Australia towards Asians still interferes with Australia's diplomatic relations with Malaysia'. The answer to my question will, in effect, be a judgment of the acceptability or otherwise of this claim; the evidence that I gather and the arguments that I read and create in trying to answer the question become premises for my eventual conclusion (which either confirms or rejects that initial claim). A question, then, can be seen as a conclusion-in-prospect: a proposed relationship between ideas that needs to be tested. The question 'What caused Australia to become less reliant on the United Kingdom in economic and political terms following the Second World War?' is different in that it presumes that Australia *did* become less reliant and that the answers will show how that occurred.

So, questions are a way of unlocking and understanding the relationships between ideas. Although we might think of the answers that flow from them as being isolated, individual 'facts' (claims), it is much more accurate to characterise the answers as *relations* between claims and, within a claim, between ideas and/or events. To ask a question is always to call on some existing knowledge and to seek the connection between the answer and that existing knowledge. We want to develop these relationships so that they can form our claims, as well as the links between premises and from premises to conclusions, in our analytical structures. Every stage in the process of analysing an issue can be thought of as one of questioning or interrogating. Questions provide the underlying 'glue' that binds together the initial formulation of the topic or problem about which we are reasoning, our search for information about that topic, and the construction of an argument or explanation that leads to a conclusion.

It is not the answers to these questions that matter, so much as the very fact that you ask them. Most students are worried about 'the right answer'; people asked to perform a certain task at work also worry about getting the right outcome. There are few (if any) perfectly correct answers in the real world; instead there are processes we go through in order to come to a conclusion (an answer or outcome) that is going to be accepted as correct in relation to the context within which we operate. And that is why reasoning is so important. Reasoning is not about answers (the conclusions), but about the process of *making answers more acceptable* by giving appropriate reasons for them. Thinking through a series of questions is how we control this process.

Hence, before and during the research process, we need to have questions in mind that are prompted by the particular topic or issue that we are investigating. We need, at the very least, to be using questions to formulate the precise dimensions of our topic—establishing the parameters of our analysis:

- what we do consider and what we do not consider
- what broadly defined bodies of knowledge we will and will not call upon
- what definitions of terms we will use within our reasoning
- what methods of investigation we will use.

In particular, we need to ask these questions to avoid assuming that there is 'one right topic' in relation to a broad issue. Often the topics we are told to investigate or write about (whether through our work or study) are poorly formed or are deliberately 'open', thus requiring us to redefine them more carefully before we work on them. Each issue we encounter can give rise to a wide variety of topics. As we go about narrowing it down to the precise topic we are going to investigate, we must always be ready to justify our choices by thinking through the fundamental question of 'Why have I chosen this particular topic, in this way, with references to these ideas and not some other topic?'. If we do, then we will able to argue for and establish the acceptability of our decisions about topics.

A precise topic enables us to search efficiently for information that will become our claims. It guides us regarding the sorts of reasoning we will need to use (reasoning from cause, analogy, and so on). A precise topic gives us a benchmark against which we can assess the relevance of any information we encounter, both in our research and in the final planning and construction of our arguments and explanations. A precise topic also provides the benchmark that enables us to judge the degree of evidence and argumentation needed to meet any requirements of the burden of proof, thus guiding our search further. But the key issue here is not the final product—the topic itself—but the insights we gain through the process of formulating it, and we must always be ready to change our topic in light of what we discover.

We will encounter some more questions in chapter 9. For the moment, let us turn to the ways in which we can think about the research process, not in terms of 'what' we will find so much as the way that information and knowledge relates to the particular topic we are reasoning about.

Information understood by where we find it

Let us begin with a little history lesson.[1] J. C. R. Licklider was a leading US scientist in the 1950s and 1960s. One of the founders of the Internet, and a visionary, he was lead author of a report in the 1960s on the future of the library, and libraries of the future. The report's main argument first of all recognised the value of the printed page. It was a superlative medium for information display and processing—'small, light, movable, cuttable, clippable, pastable, replicable, disposable, and inexpensive'. But, in an early sign of the impending crisis of information overload, the report outlined how the collecting of pages into books, journals, magazines, and bound documents, while necessary to allow even basic retrieval of information once printed, negated many or all of the display/processing features while only partially solving the huge difficulties of classifying, storing, and retrieving individual pages. It also created its own organisational problems.

Licklider concluded 'if books [and we might include here all bound collections of pages] are intrinsically less than satisfactory for the storage, organisation, retrieval, and display of information, then libraries of books are bound to be less satisfactory also'. A device, he said, was needed to allow both the transport of information to the reader 'without transporting material' and, at the same time, some processing of that information in ways that suited the reader's particular needs/uses of that information: 'a meld of library and computer is evidently required'.

While we might think we have that device—the Internet—we can probably see, even from the most cursory searching and browsing, that the Internet has solved many problems, but only at the cost of creating a lot of new problems.

I use this example to make the point that the different categories of information sources you encounter (e.g. monographs, edited collections, journals (both print and electronic), newspapers, magazines, web sites, email lists, reference books, conference proceedings, and so on) are primarily designed to assist in organising information to make it readily available, rather than to assist you immediately to decide what to use for your reasoning. They make information accessible rather than making it analytical, sensible, or useable.

That said, we should not ignore the way in which the places we look for information can, with careful use, provide some clues in the search for sense and utility. While these places might be distinguished by labels that tend to describe the form of their production (conference papers, monographs), these labels also imply certain judgments about the value and reliability of information one finds there. Here are some examples:

- *Academic conferences* are normally held to enable scholars and experts to present the latest findings of their research or applied work to their colleagues; each paper that is presented is usually no more than an hour long, often shorter. Conferences tend to be organised around a topic, or defined subject. As a result, conference proceedings will tend to contain large numbers of highly specific papers that present detailed information on very tightly defined topics; the information is usually very recent.

- *Journals* are, in many cases, designed solely or predominantly for an academic audience and the papers in them are refereed, that is, checked for quality by experts. Hundreds of journals are published; like conferences, they are tightly themed. *Media International Australia* is a premier journal, usually focusing on Australian issues concerning the media: print and electronic. Articles tend to be longer, providing academics with greater scope to explain and explore their topic; but they also serve as part of an in-depth long-term conversation among scholars and experts in various intellectual disciplines.

- *Popular magazines* are intended to be read by people without much knowledge in a particular subject, but an interest. They are, predominantly, also governed by the need to attract and retain readership. The information is heavily processed to make it understandable: simplicity, rather than complexity, is the aim; brevity ensures continued attention; examples and evidence are often sacrificed for the sake of a strong theme; research is limited.

What creates these different categories, then, is a mix of the mode of production, the intended audience and the manner of publication. We cannot, for example, make the above three distinctions without relying on the others. Journals appear as a distinct category precisely because there are other forms of publishing that are categorised differently. It is the relationship that matters. For analytical purposes, these clues provide only marginal assistance in making sense of the information, rich and complex, which we find in these sources. All they do is guide us, to some extent, as to the reliability of that information and perhaps the directness of the source (see 'Direct and indirect sources' later in this chapter). Thus, when we consider a key issue in reasoning—are our premises well founded? (chapter 5)—we can see that this foundation is provided, very often, by the source of the information. Thus, deciding what exactly to find and how to find it may not be helped by these categories, but they are important in finalising the strength and quality of argument. What we need at this stage are some other ways of thinking about how to find and use information.

Exercise 8.1

Write down all the sources that you can think of, in no particular order; perhaps start by listing the ones that you use most frequently. Then review the list and see if there are any you have missed. Remember, we are not talking here about specific titles, but types of sources. Thus, do not write '*The Australian*', write 'newspapers'. On the other hand, do not be too general: there is no point in writing 'books'; you need to ask what kind.

Information as it relates to other information

While each topic or subject on which we might conduct research will throw up its own specific relations between individual pieces of information, there are some broadly applicable general 'possibilities' of relation that can assist you in reading critically, that is, reading in a way that makes it possible to argue and explain. We have already encountered the basis for these general possibilities in chapter 7, when looking at the various ways in which we can reason. Using as my broad example here, 'the impact of the Internet on Australian society', I will give some examples of how thinking about the relationship of information to additional information might guide our search for more material.

Relations of specific and general

We might read in an article about two successful e-commerce ventures in Australia (call them x.com.au and y.com.au). Immediately we need to think: are these two specific examples unusual, representative, evidence of a trend? We are seeing if there is a relationship between the specific claim 'x and y are successful e-commerce businesses' and a more general claim that 'there are many successful e-commerce businesses in Australia'. We need to read additional articles/books to find out if there are many more examples or not.

To reverse the example, we might read that, while more men use the Internet in Australia than women, those women who are online spend more time communicating and less time surfing the web. We are trying to determine what kind of computer training needs to be given to a group of elderly women at a nursing home who are all keen to 'get online': can we relate that general information to the specific case we are investigating? Or, perhaps, we need more detailed information on what older women do (not just 'women'). Again, we go to a source looking specifically for this material, based on the tentative information-relationship we have identified.

Relations of similarity and difference

We might, for example, discover that there has been a 100 per cent increase in Internet use in Australia in the past two years. We can immediately begin to think about the following—was this increase the same, or more or less in previous years? Have there been similar rises in other countries recently?

Again, in a more complex example, we read that Australia was one of the countries that most quickly (in terms of time and number of users) adopted video recorders and mobile phones when they were introduced. There is a relationship there: both the Internet and VCRs/phones are information/communication technologies—can we draw some lessons from a comparison? Are they similar enough? Too different?

A final example: we read that the Internet cannot be easily censored; we then read another article that outlines the reasons why it can be censored effectively. The relationship here is one of difference: two conclusions that are contradictory. We need to ask: how can these two positions be resolved, if at all? Why do the authors have different perspectives on a similar theme?

Relations of cause and effect

We hear from friends that many new members of a virtual community to which they belong report initially high levels of enthusiasm, followed by a rapid decline in interest and a return to the activities that previously they pursued. We have also read, in a book on virtual communities, that this effect can be seen in many online communities. We also read, in yet another book on communities in general, that it is not the physical area nor the communication between members that makes 'a community' but the shared activities which members undertake without realising they are 'in a community'. A link seems to suggest itself: we need to look for information on the possibility that what causes the failure of virtual communities is, in some cases, the fact that the only commonality of members is the time they spend online 'doing' the community, rather than actually being it.

These are, in simplified form, examples of the way we need to make information analytical if we are to use it effectively.

Information classified by the topic under investigation

As well as looking for information prompted by how it relates to other information, we can also consider that there are, broadly, five classes of information involved in reasoning.[2] Each is defined in relation to the particular topic we are investigating, and to each other. These classes can be understood as an answer to the question 'how does this information relate to the information involved in my specific topic of investigation?'. They are:

1   information directly relating to the specific topic we are investigating
2   information about the specific background to this topic (closely related knowledge)
3   information about *other* topics, different from the specific focus of our investigation, but that provides insights that are relevant or analogous to our topic
4   information about the broad field of topics into which this particular topic fits
5   information of theoretical perspectives that are used to establish the topic as a topic and to set the parameters of investigation.

Each class denotes a different *relationship* between information, focused around the topic. For example, what allows us to talk about a 'related topics' class is the relationship between that class and the specific topic we are reading about. To even think in these terms is to be implicitly analysing the world. Let us consider an extended example of the analysis that lies behind this classification. Imagine we are investigating the way in which nationalism is used in Australian television advertising (think, for example, of the QANTAS television commercials with the 'I still call Australia home' theme or Telstra advertisements that emphasise 'We are Australian'). Here are some examples of what we might find when we are guided by the five classes above.[3]

First, we need to gather material on the *specific topic* itself. While we might well find material written in advertising magazines (such as *Ad News*), we would first watch numerous television commercials that use images of Australia. We could interview other viewers; we could talk to advertising agencies. We could compare nationalistic and other advertisements. This class of knowledge is what is usually established by the regular research activities of various scholars and investigators. So, in our own investigation, it is the principal category of knowledge that *we* are creating.

Second, we should turn to material on the *specific background*, which is usually found in the writings of other researchers. For example, Paul James's article, 'Australia in the Corporate Image: A New Nationalism'[4] discusses in detail the use of Australian nationalism in marketing campaigns in the 1970s.

Third, we need to know about other specific topics with relevant insights. Ruth Abbey and Jo Crawford's 'Crocodile Dundee or Davey Crockett?'[5] does not tell us anything about television advertising. But, in its discussion of the nationalist elements of the film *Crocodile Dundee*, we can find some relevant insights.

Fourth, we need to understand the broad background of the topic, which would involve developing our knowledge of advertising and nationalism. Benedict Anderson's *Imagined Communities: Reflections on the Origin and Spread of Nationalism*[6] includes very little discussion specifically about Australia or advertising but does provide a sophisticated discussion of nationalism. Equally, Stuart Cunningham and Graeme Turner's edited collection *The Media in Australia: Industries, Texts, Audiences*[7] provides a good general background to the 'television' side of our investigation.

Most significantly, we need to gather some information about theoretical perspectives. These perspectives provide a particular way of investigating and thinking about issues. Different theories lead researchers and thinkers to different approaches and to different understandings of what makes premises well founded, relevant, and strong. In particular, theoretical perspectives establish the topic *as a topic* and set the parameters of investigation. Remember, there are many different ways of understanding the world, which are usually related to various academic disciplines. It was not, for example, until the 1970s that cultural studies (of the popular media) became common. Each theoretical perspective will have different ideas about what exactly is an appropriate topic for investigation and how we should go about it. In broad terms, then, we could think about whether our interest in the topic is, for example, psychological or sociological. We could also think about whether we are developing, for example, a feminist or Marxist critique of this use of nationalism. Judith Williamson's classic *Decoding Advertisements: Ideology and Meaning in Advertisements*[8] provides excellent theoretical material on critiques (rather than description) of advertising. In contrast, Mark Poster's *The Mode of Information*[9] discusses the difficulties of even engaging in a 'critical' analysis of television in the 'postmodern' age. Neither book makes any reference to Australia or nationalist advertising, but both provide knowledge of the very ways in which we come to think about topics such as 'nationalist television advertising'.[10] Although the most difficult class of knowledge to analyse and engage with, knowledge about the processes of developing or discovering knowledge (what philosophers call epistemological theory), is, in fact, the general key to effective reasoning in any particular situation.

Information as it relates to how we are using it

As well as classifying information in relation to the topic we are investigating, we can also think about four *types* of information in terms of how we will use that information in our own reasoning. This typology of information answers the question 'How does this information relate to what I am trying to do in my argument or explanation?'. These four types do not 'coincide' in any way with the five classes just discussed. We can find information of any type in any of the classes just discussed; all classes can contribute to the information of one type that we are gathering.

The four main types of information are:

1   general understanding of the *context* in which we are preparing our reasoning (in effect, the context in which our text fits)
2   *opinions and conclusions* from other peoples' arguments and explanations
3   *basic details or evidence* that we need as the main source of our premises
4   *values and attitudes* (of ourselves and others) that relate to our investigation.

First of all, we need a general understanding of the context of our reasoning. It helps us to see the parameters of the topic or problem—the boundaries and overlaps between a particular topic and other related topics. Remember all 'topics' are, to some extent, artificial delineations within a swirling mass of ideas and events. Topics emerge through the ways that people think about this mass. We cannot *impose* whatever topics we want onto the world, but equally we cannot rely on the world to throw up topics 'ready-made'. Similarly, general information helps us to see how any topic can be approached from different angles with different questions to be answered. In the nationalism example you could, for example, ask 'Why do advertisers use nationalistic images and slogans?' or 'Why do people respond well to nationalistic images and slogans?'. These questions address distinctly different issues, since it may be that people do not, on the whole, respond well to such images but (for some reason) advertisers *think* they do.

This sort of general information helps us think about where and how to search for more detailed information, and to settle upon an aspect of the topic on which to concentrate. For example, in a report to a marketing firm about what people see on television, the main focus would be on the former question, rather than the latter. The context of, for example, a short lecture to high-school students would require that we keep the information in our argument or explanation consistent with their expectations and needs; if, on the other hand, we were writing a scholarly article about television advertising, then the different context would require more advanced and complex arguments. We need to gather background information in order to gain a good understanding of the context in which our reasoning takes place.

Whatever *we* may think of a particular issue, we are also looking in our research for different opinions and conclusions. For any particular topic, a range of ideas will already have been expressed, and whatever we are doing needs to take account of them. Reasoning involves acknowledging what others have done and integrating our contribution (no matter how small) with the body of knowledge already assembled. We need to criticise conclusions that we oppose, ponder those that are interesting, and add to any with which we agree. In the advertising example, we find that some critics argue that nationalistic television commercials promote unhealthy competition and suspicion of 'foreigners'. If we agree, then we should seek to substantiate this claim further. On the other hand, if, as part of our analysis, we are seeking to establish a different conclusion, we would not simply ignore this 'opposing' view, but would seek information or give arguments that refute it. We need to consider these 'other' conclusions in relation to what we are concluding in our own reasoning.

Most of all we need to base our reasoning on premises and further support for those premises. We might think of these premises as evidence or 'the facts' (even though we must understand that most 'facts' are only interpretations—claims that, depending on one's perspective, may become more or less doubtful). This information is usually what we produce through our own direct research, seeking to answer specific questions that we have established to guide our activities. As always, we need to be confident in the accuracy and acceptability of this infor-mation and be able to demonstrate it convincingly in our reasoning (for example, through appeals to authority). Referring back to our continuing example, we could use the following as evidence:

- Telecom spent over a billion dollars on all advertising in 1994, and most of the commercials had a nationalist theme.
- QANTAS consciously seeks to establish itself as a national Australian airline.
- Australians see themselves in the mould of Crocodile Dundee and other 'bush' heroes.

Yet we could also gather evidence to support any claims we make about the ways that intellectuals have previously written about advertising. For example, if our investigation includes a critique of marketing theorists' conclusions that television commercials are effective, we would need evidence, first of all, that these theorists *had* made such conclusions. When looking for evidence, then, we are not looking for a specific 'thing' but simply the material that will become the majority of our premises.

Finally, the sort of information that is most important (yet least often considered) is not actually stated in most books and articles. It remains implied, waiting within texts to be inferred by their readers. It concerns the values and attitudes of the authors of what you read and hear. These values include judgments about which actions are good and which are bad. For example, many commentators on nationalism believe that too much national pride is bad because it promotes conflict and competition. Unless we understand this value system, we cannot interpret and respond to what is written within it. We cannot understand the range of possible opinions on nationalism unless we understand that the same 'facts' (say, one particular advertisement) may lead to dramatically different conclusions when interpreted from different political or ethical standpoints. Moreover, values can also relate to 'correct' ways of investigating a problem. If we do a socio-economic analysis of television advertising in relation to the ways that large companies profit from calling upon consumers' patriotism, then, implicitly, we are making a value judgment that it is inappropriate to use a different approach (say, a psychological one that concentrates solely on how an individual responds to advertisements).

Exercise 8.2

Think about an investigation in which you are currently engaged (an essay, report, experiment, whatever). Think of two examples for each of the five classes and four types of information listed above. Remember that for each type or class, it is a question of the relation between the knowledge or information and your topic. Reflect in particular on the context in which your investigation is occurring.

Direct and indirect sources

Direct sources

In broad terms, direct sources are those that provide first-hand information about events. A radio interview with a politician in which we hear what the politician has to say about the economy is first-hand. An extensive speech delivered in Parliament by the same politician is also first-hand. A book that analyses this politician's particular views about the economy is, by contrast, second-hand. In scientific disciplines, experiments are the most common direct source; in other disciplines, surveys and interviews, or research into written and oral records of events provide direct access to information. All these sources are direct and, within the appropriate context, recognised as containing original evidence and ideas. They are a significant source of the material we need to form our arguments and explanations.

It used to be thought that these direct or 'primary' sources were somehow more 'factual' or descriptive, and that interpretation was added to them by investigators when they wrote about their research, thereby creating a 'secondary' or indirect source (see below). However, direct sources do contain values and elements of interpretation.[11] The importance of the distinction between direct and indirect sources, then, is not that one is 'fact' and the other interpretation but, rather, one of context. For example, the comments made by an advertising agency director about nationalistic television commercials must be understood in relation to the person who made these comments, why, when, how, and in what situation the comments were made, and so on. If we do an experiment by measuring the biological reactions of people watching nationalist advertising under controlled conditions, then we, in effect, become the authors of that data (via the way that we establish the experiment). We would need to ask ourselves the same sorts of questions to understand the meaning of the data we gather. By doing so, we will recognise that the contexts in which this direct 'evidence' of nationalist advertising is gathered is different to that in which we use it as part of our argument.

In every case, then, direct sources can only be used effectively when we think about the *context*, as well as the content, of the information we draw from them. Sometimes, understanding this context involves asking questions about where and when the information was produced; by whom; for what purpose; on the basis of what knowledge; in relation to which issues. Equally, the context can be understood by thinking about our own engagement with the source. For example, scientists must check, when performing experiments, that they have established the experimental procedure properly, that there are no errors in their procedures, that they are reliable observers of the events, and so on. In each discipline, in each field of endeavour, there are basic rules that we must follow, and assumptions that we must make, when seeking to gather information from direct sources; there are also basic understandings about how to consider the context of the information. They are too numerous and complex to discuss here in detail, but two examples can be drawn from history and chemistry. In history, a standard approach is to think about the way in which a person's social position (class, race, gender, and so on) can influence and be seen in what they have said or written. In chemistry, experimental design is always used to control and maintain quality of experimental work: the information gained through an experiment is always assessed in the context of the way the experiment was performed. In general terms, we must learn the rules that are part of our context and consciously apply them so that we can use direct sources effectively.

Indirect sources

As noted above, a direct source differs from an indirect source. Indirect sources involve the reports and analysis of direct information by other people. Reports, articles, and books by scholars are the main category of secondary sources that we tend to use, especially when we are beginning to develop our knowledge about an issue. Once again, the key to using such information is always to think about the context in which it was produced. In other words, information from indirect sources is only as good as our understanding of that source itself. For example, as a result of changes over the past two decades, an academic commentary such as the one by James on advertising in the 1970s may not be precisely relevant to contemporary concerns. There is no general rule to apply to such analysis of sources, except that we must always think about the context (who obtained the information; when, where, and how the information was arrived at) as well as the text (what the information is).

For example, imagine you are watching a television program on advertising. The host makes some comments on nationalistic commercials, saying that they always produce an emotional reaction and that is why they are effective. Is this source useful for an academic investigation? If you answered no, then you would, in some circumstances, be correct. But the important question to ask is 'Why?'. Let us contrast this hypothetical television program with a more usual source: academic writing. The trustworthiness of academic writing is based on the idea that the person doing the writing is an expert in that area, through their close study of the topic, their skills as a researcher, their careful, long-term analysis, and their involvement in a system in which articles and books are published only after the scrutiny of other qualified academics to determine if they are 'right' or not. In other words, the claims are trustworthy because an institutionalised method makes them trustworthy. It is a social convention that academic work is regarded as being more 'sound' (if often more remote) than 'popular' work; it is also a worthwhile social convention because there are good reasons to accept this distinction in soundness.

The usefulness of the television program depends, however, on what exactly we are trying to find. It might be quite relevant to argue that the popular *perception* of nationalist advertising is very important in the effectiveness of such commercials. So, even if we distrust many of the claims that are advanced in the popular media and trust those from more scholarly work instead, we can still use as evidence the fact that people do actually make and listen to the first sort of claim. In other words, while we may not trust the television program as an indirect commentary on advertising, we could certainly use it as a direct source of popular views on advertising.

Do you see the difference? Sometimes we will want to make claims in our reasoning that convey information in the claims themselves. And sometimes we will want to make claims about the fact that a certain type of claim, or group of claims, has been made by others. Developing the latter type of writing is essential in good critical work and, thus, requires you to develop skills in knowing about sources of knowledge.

Exercise 8.3

Write a short analysis of the different direct and indirect sources that you use most frequently in your current reasoning. What questions do you need to ask about them? What rules and assumptions, stemming from the discipline or profession in which you are working or studying, underlie the identification of these sources?

Five possible outcomes

Finding information effectively is, in large measure, a matter of understanding how that information or knowledge is to be used in your own arguments and explanations. Often we simply want some basic descriptive information to serve as claims in our reasoning without wanting to provide extensive supporting arguments. For instance, we read, in relation to our nationalistic advertisements investigation, that *Crocodile Dundee* was one of the most popular films ever screened in Australia. We can simply state this piece of information, either quoting exactly from the original or re-expressing the information in our own words, giving an appropriate reference to it.[12] We are simply taking a single claim from our 'source'.

We can also take an entire argument or explanation from our 'source'. We could quote such reasoning exactly, but usually, for stylistic reasons, we express it in our own words. For example, James's article (mentioned above) argues that nationalistic advertisements encourage consumers to purchase a corporation's products because, by being 'Australian' (even when the companies are often owned by foreign interests), the products are assumed to be better than others. We are, in effect, getting claims *and* links (reasoning) from the 'source' (can you see the trace of linking in 'because'?). Once again, we provide a reference in order to acknowledge our debt to the original author.

Yet very often what we want to 'take' from these sources is not that specific and cannot simply be 'found' by looking at a certain page. Instead, we can summarise the basic argument or explanation in a source that we have read (always in our own words), reducing a long text to a short series of premises and a conclusion, which we can then use in our own argument (again, with an appropriate reference). For example, Anderson's *Imagined Communities* is a long and detailed work on nationalism that, in part, concludes that technologies that allow humans to overcome geographical distance (for example, railways) have played a significant role in the creation of modern nations. We could include such a summary (which, of course, can be expressed in the analytical format in our notes) within our own reasoning. We are, thus, taking from the source not a specific claim, nor a specific piece of reasoning, but our *understanding* (analytically speaking) of the source's overall argument or explanation.

Fourth, we can take from sources a type of information that is far more indefinable than the information gained in any of the last three cases. This category can be summed up as 'positions and values'. It is usually hidden within the source and can be recovered using your judgment (based on what you read or hear) of the underlying position that the author of the source holds. This underlying position can be inferred from that person's own arguments or explanations, or the way in which the arguments or explanations have been received by others. We read, for example, in Graeme Turner's *Making It National*[13] that Australian businesses exploit national patriotism and sentiment to further their own profit-making goals. Whether we agree or disagree with this conclusion, whether we can refute it or not, we can nevertheless try to understand why he might have made such a conclusion. We can ask, what is the political and intellectual position that is implied by such claims? From the overall thrust of Turner's analysis, we judge that he is opposed to unfettered capitalism, seeking instead a greater degree of regulation in the national interest. In making this judgment, we can understand the assumptions that underlie the information in Turner's book, and the context in which it was written and presented to us. Without such analysis, you will always tend to respond to reasoning from your own point of view, without understanding why others might disagree with you. Whether or not you wish to change their minds or accept their right to be different is immaterial: neither goal can be achieved if you do not know why they believe what they do.

Finally, there are occasions on which we take *nothing* away from what we are reading or observing—except more questions! This outcome may be frustrating at times, but if we are seeking to be smart thinkers, we must be prepared to delve deeply into an issue and not rush too quickly to a satisfying answer. Remember analysis continues through every stage of research, but smart thinkers are aware of this and draw encouragement from the way in which a book that tells you 'nothing' might prompt the question 'Why does it not tell me anything?'. And, further, you can ask if the problem is with the book, with you, or perhaps with your original set of analytical questions.

Exercise 8.4

Using a long piece of written work that you are reading at the moment, practise getting each of the five possible outcomes just discussed. Make sure that, in each case, you express your answers in the analytical structure format (except, of course, for the last category, for which you will simply have a list of further questions).

Review

We have seen in previous chapters how the context in which we create our texts of reasoning are crucial in making successful judgments about the effective-ness of our arguments and explanations. In this chapter, we have concentrated on learning about the process of searching for knowledge in a way that allows us to take the information *from* one context (someone else's text) and put it *into* another context (our text). The context influences our interpretation and understanding of information, and so if we do not understand and recognise these contexts, our analysis will not be sound. Knowledge, then, needs to be understood generically, not as specific 'facts' or issues, but as a series of classes and types that relate to our research project. The sources from which it comes, again, must be analysed for the way they create and constrain that knowledge, rather than as particular books or articles or experiments. Finally, what we take away from these sources can be organised as elements of reasoning: as claims, arguments, or explanations; as assumptions and values; or simply as more questions.

CONCEPT CHECK

The following terms and concepts are introduced in this chapter. Before checking in the Glossary, write a short definition of each term:

analysis

analytical questions

information

knowledge

source

Review exercise 8

Answer briefly the following questions giving, where possible, an example in your answer that is different from those used in this book:

a. What do we need to know to be good researchers?
b. What sorts of questions are involved in formulating a topic?
c. What allows us to classify information into five separate categories?
d. How do the four types of information compare and contrast with each other?
e. What is the difference between a direct and an indirect source?
f. What role does the 'author' and the mode of production of information play?
g. What are the important issues of context involved in using information from any source?
h. Why must we ask questions when we are searching?

NOTES

1 This information, and quotes from Licklider's report, are taken from Mark Stefik, *Internet dreams: archetypes, myths, and metaphors*, MIT Press, Cambridge, Mass., 1996, pp. 23–32.
2 Please note that my classifying of information here is just one of many different approaches which you may encounter. I have developed it because it usefully extends our smart thinking abilities and not because it is 'right' in any objective sense.
3 All these examples are drawn from the process of researching and writing that went into

M. Allen, 'Telecom Adverts, Telecom Networks, Telecom Australia', *Australian Journal of Communication*, vol. 20, no. 2, 1993, pp. 97–113.

4 *Arena*, no. 63, 1983, pp. 65–106.
5 *Meanjin*, vol. 46, no. 2, 1987, pp. 145–52.
6 Verso, London, 1981.
7 Allen & Unwin, Sydney, 1993.
8 Marion Boyars, London, 1978.
9 University of Chicago Press, Chicago, 1990.
10 These sorts of theoretical insights into the intellectual issues involved in any research or analysis often appear within more general discussions of various topics. These examples simply indicate that the purpose of looking at the two books noted was precisely to gain this sort of knowledge.
11 There is, of course, philosophical argument about this issue. See chapter 9 for a brief discussion of the intersubjective theory of knowledge that underpins this view of direct sources.
12 In this case, the authority is S. Crofts, 'Re-Imaging Australia: Crocodile Dundee Overseas', *Continuum*, vol. 2, no. 2, 1989, p. 133.
13 Allen & Unwin, Sydney, 1995.

9

Planning and Creating Your Reasoning

Although, in practice, reasoning, knowledge, research, and analysis are all inextricably bound together, it is also true that, from time to time, we divide our reasoning tasks up in a way that allows us to sit down and prepare an analytical text containing arguments and explanations. What we have learnt about reasoning so far makes us much more effective in such preparation, and this chapter briefly discusses two ways in which we can go about it. However, always remember that the key to good reasoning is not a 'method' or program of steps to follow but an *attitude*—a keenness to think things through. The advice that follows is designed principally to 'jog' your mind into this sort of keenness and should be applied judiciously, on the basis of the particular skills and needs that apply to you as an individual smart thinker.

In this chapter:

1 We will consider some of the key questions that can help us determine the external context in which our argument or explanation fits. Then, revisiting the planning method from chapter 3, we will look at the questions that are most useful in guiding the reasoning in the text we are preparing.

2 We conclude with a short example of the way that the analytical structure format can be used, not to represent our entire argument and explanation, but instead as a 'plan' of ideas and relationships that can then be used to assist in actually writing the narrative flow of our reasoning.

The key analytical questions

Context: analysing the external dimensions of reasoning

Throughout this book, we have seen how context is all-important in determining many of our judgments about effective reasoning. When planning and creating (and then presenting) an argument or explanation, the particular context in which this reasoning occurs must be actively considered. The nature of context—a mass of implied or assumed knowledge and expectations—makes it impossible for us to develop precise guidelines for its consideration. Instead, we must explore the three-way relationship between the person or people creating reasoning (the author), the people receiving this reasoning (the audience), and the knowledge that this reasoning uses and develops.

Reasoning is about the use, expression, and formation of knowledge, and involves innumerable judgments about the 'truth' of claims and the 'truth' of the way they link to one another in various reasoned ways. Knowledge does not exist objectively in the world (literally in the 'objects' that claims represent). Rather it is created intersubjectively, that is, between people such as authors and their audiences (known, technically, as 'subjects').[1] Knowledge (consisting of claims and their relationships) *does have* an objective element, since it represents, in another form, the actual reality of objects. However, the medium of that representation—the form in which knowledge is expressed—is language, which (unfortunately, perhaps) is *not* a perfectly representational medium. Whenever we write or talk about things ('objects'), we add to or subtract from their essential nature through the particular choice of words we use. Hence claims, and all knowledge built from those claims, are always something more or less than what 'really' happens.

All humans share a common reality and appear, through the words they use (when properly translated), to have a common language to discuss and think about it. But remember that language consists not only of the descriptive or denotative characteristic of words but also of their *connotative* function (the way in which they carry implied meanings). These connotations ensure that we cannot assume that knowledge always and perfectly matches up to reality. Knowledge will always be constrained by and, in part, created from the words in which it is expressed. Moreover, the implied values and assumed knowledge that make words meaningful exist through the interactions of people—the authors and audiences of reasoning. That is why knowledge is intersubjective. Moreover, it is not simply a question of thinking about individuals: who 'we' are as subjects depends very much on the culture and society in which we grow up and, indeed, the knowledge that we already possess. Hence, whenever we think about ourselves as authors of reasoning or about our potential audiences, we are thinking about cultural and social assumptions and expectations about knowledge and reasoning.

The aim here is not to gain a detailed understanding of the philosophical arguments for or against objective or intersubjective knowledge; it is to understand that all reasoning involves people and that, hence, knowledge and reasoning can never completely escape the influence of the social contexts in which those people exist and operate. Even if philosophical ideas about intersubjectivity are unfamiliar, their practical effects should be apparent. Have you ever been in a situation in which, despite the apparent 'logic' and 'certainty' of your argument, those listening to you have failed to agree with your conclusion? Have you ever been asked to learn something without understanding why you are learning it? Have you ever written a report or essay and been pleased with what you have done, only to be told by its readers that you have not done what was required of you? These situations come about when the author and audience of reasoning fail to work within a shared context of assumptions and expectations.

This context can be understood by thinking through the following questions about our own work (many of which we encountered in chapter 8 in relation to others' reasoning). Forget, for a moment, *what* we are reasoning about and think instead about the following questions:

- Why am I reasoning?
- For whom am I reasoning?
- In what situation is my reasoning taking place?
- According to what methods, definitions, and broad understandings am I reasoning?
- What is expected of me?

Knowing what context we are working within may involve 'fitting in' with what our audience expects and assumes, or it can require us to outline and discuss possible alternative contexts explicitly, thereby helping our audience to fit in with the context that *we* want to establish.

Here is one example of the importance of context. HIV/AIDS is generally regarded as one of the world's great health risks. We know certain things about the virus that causes AIDS, such as its methods of transmission (through blood and other bodily fluids) and the types of activities that enable this transmission (e.g. unprotected sex and intravenous drug use with shared needles). We also know what it does to human beings (destroys their immune system and indirectly causes their death). Now, as far as we can tell, these claims are objectively 'true'. Yet, think of the different sets of assumptions about, say, how to stop unprotected sex that would *not* be shared by a Western health expert and, say, a group of politicians from a conservative Islamic community. The Westerner, with a background of social freedom and individual choice, would be full of ideas about advertising campaigns and other strategies to encourage people to use condoms; the Islamic community leaders would be bemused by this approach—even actively hostile— since their framework of assumptions does not include such liberal attitudes to sex, nor does it include the use of condoms. Neither party is wrong here: it is neither rational nor irrational to hold either of these two sets of assumptions, as long as each fits in with the accepted practices of the community to which it belongs. Yet the possibility for misunderstanding is great, *unless* both parties make an effort to understand the assumptions of the other and try to find some common ground from which to engage in the specific argument about HIV. While the final resolution of such a clash of frameworks does not necessarily mean 'sticking with' one's original assumptions, effective reasoning requires that the difference be acknowledged and explained properly before any moment of resolution.

Exercise 9.1

In relation to an issue that you are working on at the moment, write down a series of questions that will help you to establish the external dimensions of your topic (how it relates to the general audiences and knowledge of your reasoning).

Text: the internal dimensions of reasoning

Chapter 3 introduced the idea of a particular planning method, which revolves around the use of the analytical structure format. Here, as a reminder, are the five steps involved in this method:

1   Decide what your conclusion will be. Write this claim out carefully, expressing exactly what you mean. Number it '1'.
2   Then think about the reasons that you are giving for this conclusion. These reasons must be written as proper claims, this time serving as premises that either explain how that conclusion comes about or show why it should be accepted. Try to keep related premises together, but as the diagram will show these relationships clearly, it is not essential to group them perfectly. Write them out, making sure that you do not use pronouns but express each claim so that it makes sense in and of itself. Number them from '2' onwards. Focus on giving the main reasons for the conclusion at this stage.
3   Begin to draw the diagram to show the relationships between the claims.
4   Stop and think: are you missing any claims? do you need more premises? have you got the relationships the way you want them to be?
5   Make changes if required, adding claims and redrawing the diagram if need be.

We can learn more about each step in the process by thinking through some of the questions that we might ask to guide us in completing each step effectively. The following discussion does not, of course, cover every aspect of all situations, but will give you a general overview of the sorts of smart-thinking 'moves' we can make in planning and creating our arguments and explanations. Moreover, although this overview is broken up into specific advice about each step of the process, the actual application of the ideas discussed will obviously occur in a variety of ways, at a variety of different stages of your research and analysis. In practice, no step is isolated from the others, even if, in theory, we can distinguish them in order to learn more about them.

First, think about the conclusion, which is a specific statement of what we are going to be reasoning towards. It will relate to the general topic with which we are concerned but must be much more precise. Ask yourself:

- What is the conclusion?
- What are its specific elements (meanings of words, key ideas, values, scope, and certainty)?
- Is it about the present, future, or past?
- Does it require an argument or an explanation?
- How does it relate to existing 'conclusions' about this topic: is it opposing them? supporting them? extending them?
- Is the conclusion well formed?
- What sorts of evidence will be required to support such a conclusion?
- Is there more than one conclusion involved here, and can they be combined in some manner?

In particular, be clear about the following question:

- Is this conclusion directly about some event, decision, or issue, or is it about the way others think and write about such events, decisions, or issues?

Take, for example, the following conclusion:

1. The Olympic games are organised and run for the profit of the large corporations who televise, sponsor, and advertise the games.

This conclusion is distinctly different from the 'normal' conclusions we draw about the games but is not completely 'new'. There are some important 'issues' here, for example, issues relating to how these corporations might have gained control over an apparently 'international' event. Another issue would involve considering why the profit aspect seems to be ignored by much reporting on the games. Much evidence will be needed to explore and explain these issues; the claim will definitely require an argument to support it because (as far as I can tell) this claim is not widely accepted. It will necessarily involve discussion of others' opinions but is not, of itself, a conclusion about someone else's view.

Second, think about the main reasons. Make some initial statements of these reasons, answering questions such as:

- Why does or should the event or idea under discussion occur or be believed?
- When does it occur?
- How does it happen?
- What does it mean that this event or idea occurs or is believed?
- What are or should be the consequences?

Then, considering each reason in turn, think about the complexities of the reasons, expanding them into a chain of premises that not only expresses the reason fully but also clearly explicates how the premises relate to the conclusion. Ask yourself:

- Do the reasons need any definitions or framing premises?
- Is the relevance of the premises to the conclusion well established?

- Do the premises cover all the aspects of the conclusion?
- Are these premises well formed, with particular reference to the internal connections which they make?
- Are they well founded (if not, then what support can they be given)?
- Are enough reasons given to meet the requirements for breadth?
- Are they expanded sufficiently to give depth to the argument/explanation?
- Is each idea in the conclusion referred to in some way in these premises?
- Are the premises grouped together properly?

Just one example would be to state the following reason:

The Olympic games are now very expensive to organise.

This might break down, on further analysis, into claims such as:

2. There are more sports, more athletes, and more coaches than ever before.
3. Hosting all these events and people is very costly.
4. Non-sport costs, associated with security and entertainment, are now much more prominent.

(There are, of course, many more possible premises.)

Third, think about the analytical relationships between the premises and the conclusion (as seen in the diagram). Here, we can think about the sort of reasoning that is being used:

- Do the premises show the cause of an effect? (If so, are differences or similarities clearly stated?)
- Do they state some generalisation that provides the knowledge we need about a specific conclusion? (If so, is the specific case really a member of the general category?)
- Do the premises draw together specific cases so as to make a generalisation? (If so, are these specific cases representative of the general category?)
- Is it an analogical relationship, in which similarities between the events described in the premises and the conclusion provide the answers we are seeking? (If so, are the events consistent with one another?)
- Is it simply reasoning from terms, with the claim simply establishing the particular meaning of the conclusion? (If so, are we making it clear?)

In each case, remember that these questions unlock relationships. We can analyse events by thinking about 'What is the cause of X?' or 'What effects does X cause?'; we can think about the way that many cases of X might prompt us to generalise, or about how X might only be explicable as a specific case of some general rule.

Continuing the previous example, the premises concerning cost are about the cause of the increased commercialism of the games. Because of the need for money to fund the games (a result of these costs), there is no way they could be staged without corporate funding. Good reasoning would involve checking to see if it really is the case that increased costs is the only factor; in doing so, we might find that government funding of the Olympics has declined in the current era of low public financing and increased privatisation:

5.   There is no other source of funds for the Olympics.

As we know, premises are, by themselves, unlikely to be well founded without some authority or further reasoning. So, at this stage, we can also add further layers to our diagram, providing more claims that show or explain our premises. We can add as many layers as we wish, though for practical reasons we might wish to stop at three or four layers (see below). In each case, remember that we are using the claim at the bottom of each vertical arrow as a conclusion, and so all of the thinking moves involved in making good links between the main conclusion and its main premises also apply to these relationships.

Again, claim 4 of the Olympics example—'Non-sport costs, associated with security and entertainment, are now much more prominent'—would need to be properly supported by its own explanation, which would involve a *similar* process in which we think of a reason and then break it down into specific claims. These supporting claims might be:

6.   The Olympic games are now a prime target for terrorists.
7.   Terrorism is common in the contemporary world.
8.   Each new Olympic games tries to outdo the previous one in terms of entertainment and spectacle.
9.   Every new and different approach to entertainment usually involves greater cost.

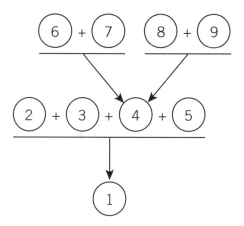

The fourth and fifth steps, which involved stopping, reflecting, and revising, are crucial. At this point we must think through the following questions, beginning also to relate our own reasoning to the context in which we are operating:

•   What assumptions underlie the reasoning?
•   Are there any implied premises?

- Is the relevance of each premise clear?
- Do they provide sufficient support to satisfy the burden of proof?
- Are all the claims well founded (either self-evidently, or with authority, or with reasoning)?
- Are the claims clear and understandable?
- Is there coherence between the scope and certainty of premises and conclusions?
- What issues are not covered by the argument as it stands? (And should they be included?)
- Is it clear why some reasons are not being considered?
- Are the value judgments in this reasoning clearly outlined and argued for?

Exercise 9.2

Using the same issue that you worked on in exercise 9.1, write down a series of questions that will help you to establish the internal dimensions of your topic (how premises relate to one another and to the conclusion; how further claims relate to the premise; and so on).

Using the analytical structure for planning
Different sorts of plans

Usually, when we are told to plan our arguments and explanations, we are given advice about how to create a good narrative flow or sequence. For example, many excellent books on writing discuss the need to plan written work so that we move from the introduction through each of the main points to the conclusion. For each stage of the work, these books give advice about what is required to make the resulting essay or report readable and effective. These books also refer to the idea of 'mind-mapping', in which, rather than trying to write down our thoughts and ideas in a linear sequence (as they will appear in final written form), we should begin by 'mapping' them all over a piece of paper, drawing lines to connect them together and adding new ideas that expand on what is already there.

Both planning methods have their advantages but only if we use them at the right time, with a clear understanding of their purpose, and knowing what each represents. They share one important feature: by externalising thoughts, that is, putting them on paper, they enable us to reflect and think through what it is we are doing. A written sequence plan should be developed last, just before we commence writing. The purpose is similar, really, to the table of contents in this book. The narrative plan guides us and reminds us what, in turn, we need to write about within the narrative sequence. It represents, in summary form, the order in which we are going to write our narrative. A mind-map should be used first, before we have really begun to think about what exactly we want to argue or explain. Its purpose is to aid us in 'brainstorming' the jumbled mass of ideas and possible connections—to get them down on paper so we can think more clearly about them. It represents the initial 'pool' of knowledge in our

heads that needs to be thought through, researched, and organised in some way before
it makes sense to others. Here is an example, covering the same topic as the analytical
structure just given.

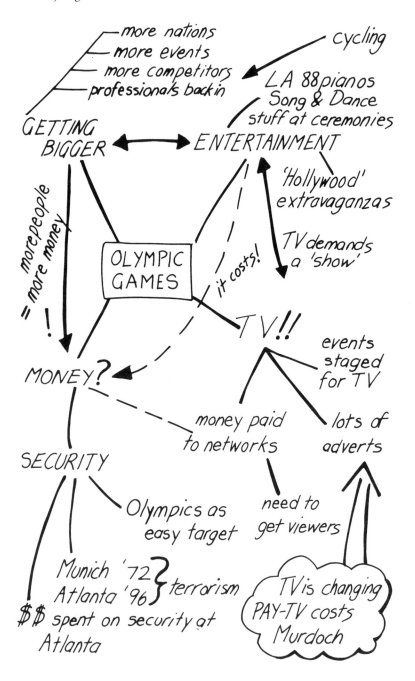

The analytical structure format as a plan for writing

The analytical structure format is different from (and, for purposes of smart thinking, much better than) a mind-map or narrative plan. The ideas that underpin it are used as the basis of the analytical questions that will guide every stage of thinking, researching, and writing. The actual written-on-paper format, with its list of claims and diagram, is then used, after initial research but before we think about the narrative sequence. It can either guide further research or guide the actual writing or presentation of our argument or explanation. It allows us to externalise the analytical relationships between ideas that are the heart of reasoning. Once on paper, these relationships and ideas (the diagram and the claims) can be checked to see what mistakes we are making, where more work needs to be done, how well we are analysing the issues, and so on.

Now, throughout this book we have been using the analytical structure format mainly as a way of understanding better what goes on within arguments and explanations. When we use it as a planning tool, we need to be careful that it does not 'take over' our project and become an end in itself. Always remember that, like any planning tool, the analytical structure format simply provides another way of helping to clarify and express your ideas in a form that assists you to complete the final task: writing the full, narrative expression of your reasoning. We must make sure that what is written in the plan can be easily translated into this final product.

With this in mind, I will use an example from chapter 6 to show how a written essay or report might develop from an analytical structure plan:

1. University education should be free for all Australians.
2. A well-educated population is more productive at work.
3. Higher productivity at work benefits the economy.
4. If something benefits the economy, then the government should encourage it.
5. The best way for the government to encourage Australians to be well educated is to provide free university education.
6. In our complex technological society, one requires university study in order to be well educated.
7. Free education is a fundamental democratic right.
8. Australia is a democracy.
9. Education includes all levels from primary to tertiary.
10. Any cost that the government imposes on people attending higher education will probably reduce the numbers attending.
11. If numbers are reduced, then Australians are obviously not being encouraged to attend.

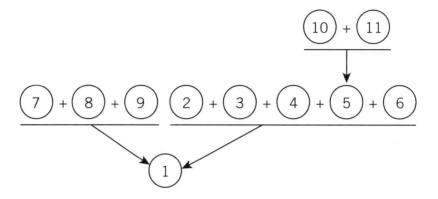

My conclusion (claim 1) is what I want my audience to agree with. Hence, I will state it clearly in the first paragraph of my narrative flow (although there are also times when it is better to leave the conclusion-claim until later on in the narrative flow).[2] At the same time, I want to signal to my readers that I will be giving them two key reasons for accepting this conclusion—these reasons are expressed, first, in claims 2–6 and, second, in claims 7–9. However, I would not go into detail in this first paragraph but would simply indicate that, broadly, I will be discussing free education in terms of economic benefit and democratic rights.

Next, although it is not represented anywhere in the analytical structure just given, I would probably give a summary or overview of the history of higher education in Australia, providing an outline of the times at which education has and has not been free. To do this properly might involve the development of a second structure diagram that captures the main points I want to make. I would also need to establish a context for this argument: I could perhaps identify it as a response to the continued pressure from the federal government to reduce public spending in favour of more private spending by individual Australians. This section of the written report (which, in this example, would be between ten and twelve pages, or 3000 words, in total) might be between two and three pages long.

Then I would begin my actual analysis by discussing the second of my two reasons (the 'democratic rights' one), since it is, for me, more significant than the 'economic benefit' reason. I would begin by writing about claim 8—'Australia is a democracy'—and would not expend too much effort on showing why I made this claim (since it is generally accepted). Probably a paragraph would be sufficient. My discussion of claim 7—'Free education is a fundamental democratic right'—is a different matter. I could expect to write between four and five paragraphs exploring every aspect of this claim, in effect developing an argument for its acceptability. I would need to consider the issue of 'rights' and what they mean; whether or not free education is a 'fundamental' right or just an added benefit where it is possible. You can see how it may well be necessary for me to stop and, thinking through my argument, develop another analytical structure in which claim 7 is the conclusion. Finally, claim 9—'Education includes all levels from primary to tertiary'—might simply be presented as a definition and expressed quickly in one or two sentences in the final written form. Alternatively, it could become a significant issue to develop further. I could perhaps show how, historically, government policy on education has developed, first with the provision of free primary education, then free secondary education for some years, then a full six years of free secondary education, and then, in the 1970s and first half of the 1980s, free tertiary education. Such a discussion might help me, later, to show the truth of claim 6—'In our complex technological society, one requires university study in order to be well educated'.

At this stage in the written format, I would probably remind my readers of the conclusion and introduce the 'economic benefit' reason, explicitly indicating that the assumptions behind it (that the government should not simply fund all democratic benefits for its citizens but should only pay for those that are economically significant) come from a different philosophical position. While the two reasons overlap to some degree, I need to make it clear that they are, essentially, quite distinct. This part of the written report would be complex and lengthy. Looking at the structure, I see that claims 2, 3, and 6 tend to be more closely related than claims 4 and 5. Hence, although logically all of these five premises are dependent on one another, I would break up my analysis into two sections and deal with each subgroup in turn. Knowing that the second subgroup (claims 4 and 5) is the crucial framing or value-judging part of the argument, I would be particularly detailed in arguing these premises through, drawing on claims 10 and 11 to make out my case for claim 5. The final part of the written work would simply restate the key reasons and the conclusion.

Here is the narrative sequence in plan form to emphasise the difference between these two planning tools:

Introduction
- Give main conclusion (1) and key reasons: economic benefit (2–6) and democratic right (7–9)

Main body: Background
- Give background on history of education in Australia with respect who paid and why.
- Provide context (the current situation that leads to this argument).

Main body 2: develop 'democratic right' reason
- Write 1 paragraph on 8; 4–5 paragraphs on 7; 4–5 paragraphs on 9.

Main body 3: Develop 'economic benefit' reason
- Distinguish this reason from previous one; signal two related aspects (2 paragraphs).
- Write 2–3 paragraphs on 2 and 3; 2–3 paragraphs on 6 (relate back to second section).
- Write 4–5 paragraphs on 5; including discussion of 10 and 11; 2–3 paragraphs on 4.

Conclusion.
- Sum up the two reasons and restate 1.

Exercise 9.3

Apply the questions developed in the first section of this chapter to the argument just outlined about higher education in Australia. What do you think of the reasoning? Is it strong? weak? Can it be improved? challenged? Write additional claims, with appropriate diagrams, that either improve on, counter, or further explore the issues raised in this argument. Then think about the general use of these analytical questions and structures in relation to your own reasoning: how can they help you to be a better smart thinker?

Review

Since reasoning is about knowledge, we must think about the epistemologies (philosophies of knowledge) that underpin the relationship between text and context. Questions can reveal the external boundaries of our topic and how it relates to other topics, knowledge, or audiences; questions can also reveal important aspects of our topic itself. The questioning process is not a 'once-off' task that we complete and then forget: it is a continuous process that relates specifically to the way in which we set down our ideas in the analytical structure format.

This structure is most useful as a planning tool and differs from usual plans, which either involve unstructured concepts (mind-maps) or ideas arranged in the order that we will write them (a narrative sequence plan). The key advantage of the analytical structure format is that it lays out, in advance of writing or presentation, the structure of key claims and the links between them in a way that is driven by the analysis—the reasoning—rather than by the way we will present the argument or explanation.

CONCEPT CHECK

The following terms and concepts are introduced in this chapter. Before checking in the Glossary, write a short definition of each term:

intersubjective

mind-map

narrative sequence plan

objective

relativism

Review exercise 9

Answer briefly the following questions giving, where possible, an example in your answer that is different from those used in this book:

a. What are the factors we need to consider if we are to understand the external dimensions of our text?
b. What are the factors we need to consider if we are to understand the internal dimensions of our text?
c. How does context affect text and vice versa?
d. What is the difference between an objective and an intersubjective philosophy of knowledge?
e. Why is it important to consider the connotative element of our claims?
f. What general purpose do plans fulfil?
g. What is the primary advantage of the analytical structure format when used for planning?
h. What are the key differences between a narrative sequence plan, a mind-map, and an analytical structure format?

NOTES

1   Some philosophers would maintain that knowledge can be objective, in those circumstances in which the knowledge is not affected at all by human subjectivity. I would contend that, while theoretically possible, this objective status is never reached in practice. Although we may, as thinking human subjects, be able to utilise methods and approaches that eliminate all possibility of subjective bias (and most academic disciplines have a wide range of such methods and approaches), the very use of these methods and approaches itself creates a subjective element. For example, within Western scientific medical practice, knowledge of diseases may be objective; however, from a different viewpoint (such as, for example, traditional or folk medicine), the very decision to use a scientific approach is itself a subjective element. Moreover, the human subject is created in part by what he or she knows. To say that knowledge is intersubjective means all knowledge is interrelated and that the specific pattern of relationship will depend upon who, when, where, and how subjects express and receive knowledge.
2   Remember that we often refer to the last paragraph of an essay or presentation as the 'conclusion'. Here, of course, because we are talking analytically, the conclusion is the key claim that we want our audience to accept.

10

Bringing It All Together: Narrative and Structure

In this final chapter, I provide a fully worked example of a substantial written argument, which I have cast and commented upon, so as to demonstrate the way in which the main form in which we encounter reasoning—the narrative flow—is perhaps better understood as an expression of an underlying process of linking premises and conclusions. This longer example also demonstrates in more detail how you might end up writing something based on an analytical structure, pointing out the subtleties of expression that provide a structure and meaning surrounding that logical core.

First, read the example, which is an argument I use to convince students of the need to reference properly when they write essays. Second, read carefully my analysis of the logic, broken down paragraph by paragraph (you might even want to try casting it yourself). Third, look at the way I try to capture the essence of the text in a simpler argument. Finally, consider my overall assessment of the ten paragraphs that make up this text.

Example text
The value of referencing

One of the problems that confronts teachers of first-year university units each semester is the need to ensure that students learn, quickly, the methods and skills of correct referencing. In some courses, students are very much left to fend for themselves, relying on, perhaps, the services of the university library, advice offered by individual staff members, or simply muddling through on the basis of critical feedback on their first assignments. The Department of Media and Information (DMI), along with some other areas of the university, takes a different approach. DMI, in its first-year unit MCI 101: Research and Presentation Project, directly addresses the need that students have to learn correct referencing techniques, devoting some weeks and an assignment to that task. Students can also practise these techniques in the assignments required in other first-year units.

Nevertheless, even when direct attention of the kind just outlined has been paid to referencing, some students continue to struggle with it. The problem is not merely a technical one, since all the students at university are capable of learning to follow the kinds of technical directions that lay out the appropriate steps needed to reference their work. What then is the cause of this problem? DMI would suggest that many students (including some who are quite able referencers) remain confused about the admittedly complex set of reasons that explain why referencing is so important in all kinds of written communication. This paper will outline these reasons before ending with a short exploration of why they might be hard for some students to grasp.

As just indicated, there are three main reasons why referencing is important in essays, reports, presentations, theses, articles, and all the other kinds of scholarly writing in which students engage both at university and then, as graduates, in their professions. Without seeking to assign a priority to any of them they are: first, that referencing enables a reader to seek out more information on the topic of the written work, based on the references given; second, referencing acknowledges authors' ethical and academic debt of thanks to those sources which they have used to create their own 'source' of information; and third, referencing provides a method by which authors can establish the validity and strength of their claims by relying on the authority of the source to which they are referring. Let us examine these reasons in more detail.

The process of effective scholarship (finding, analysing, and communicating information) involves an almost-constant acquisition of ideas, knowledge, views, and general contextual understanding. One method of finding the material from which to acquire this information, used mainly at times of intensive research, is to follow the leads provided in an article or book via the references to find, quickly and with a high degree of reliability, additional valuable, relevant sources of information. A well-constructed piece of scholarly writing will contain both information in its own right and information that assists readers in further information acquisition. Thus an author needs to see referencing as a service to the reader of their work and, using the kinds of standard methods that are available (such as the APA system), make sure readers are easily able to go from their text to others via those references.

The second reason noted above was that authors owe a debt to those writers who have provided them with information, inspiration, and ideas. This debt is both scholarly and ethical. What do I mean by assigning two different aspects to this notion of debt? Following the 'debt' metaphor through a little further, it is possible to say first that the scholarly community within which an author writes enforces payment of the debt (their readers will check their work, either consciously or not, for evidence that proper referencing has taken place). Second, it is enforced, or at least made possible, by the ethical behaviour of individual authors who, privately, must recognise they need to acknowledge those other writers who have helped them. Without referencing, the system of mutual obligation on authors to use each others' work, to link new pieces of work to those already published, and to rely on one another's specific expertise would collapse. Thus referencing is important, even if the references were never actually followed up (though, of course, they regularly are).

The third reason why referencing is so important is, perhaps, the most difficult to grasp. References allow an author to obviate the need to detail and support every single premise in their arguments and explanations by relying instead on the authority of the source from which they obtained the information they are presenting (see Allen, *Smart Thinking*, chapter 6 for more explanation). Put simply, references are part of the way one writes a convincing argument or explanation. Since good writing always seeks to be convincing, even if to only a small degree, then it is easy to see why the quest to teach students to be good writers must also involve teaching them to reference effectively.

These three reasons can be summed up as follows. Each newly produced essay, article, presentation, or whatever, is always based substantially in existing published or presented material and becomes a part of the 'ongoing, knowledgeable conversation' expressed through that material. Written work needs good referencing so as to refer its readers elsewhere, to repay the debt to other writers, and to reinforce its own arguments.

But what makes it hard for some students to grasp the essential elements of this relatively simple argument as to why they must reference, even as they dutifully follow out the instructions to 'reference correctly' laid out for them by teachers? Without going into detail, it seems likely that many students do not yet believe themselves to be authors, with an audience, and a comradeship with other authors. They see themselves primarily as students, governed by a debilitating and unequal regime of inequality in relation to their teachers. Thus, the reasons I have just outlined are not rejected by some students because they are not understood, or are unreasonably or wilfully ignored. Rather the reasons are rejected because they are, quite rationally, not relevant to a 'student', even if they are explained to students. A 'student' (by which I mean the abstract identity rather than any particular individual) is governed by the imperatives of 'doing as one is told' by teachers; a student's audience is their assessor; a student's sense of comradeship is with other students as students; the goal of writing is not, usually, 'contributing to human knowledge' but getting a good mark.

Students in general then fail to understand the need to reference because they do not see how the very sensible arguments in favour of referencing apply to them. Thus, in terms of the cultural understanding of student identity—of 'who students believe themselves to be'—we can see that students probably fail to reference effectively because they are not motivated by genuine self-interest as writers, but instead by the dubious and failure-prone motivation of obedience.

The problem with which I began this paper, namely the need to ensure that students learn, quickly, the methods and skills of correct referencing, is often addressed at university simply in a technical fashion. But, in light of the very brief analysis of the student-as-student (rather than student-as-writer) that I have just proposed, the real solution lies in a combination of effective technical help and, at least as importantly, a conscious and supportive effort to encourage students to think in new ways about themselves and the relationship they have to their teachers. Unless a relationship can develop between teachers and students that emphasises a shared (but still, by differences in experience and training, unequal) responsibility for production of knowledge, then referencing will continue to be a confusing and potentially antagonistic battleground for all concerned.

Casting and notes on each paragraph

One of the problems that confronts teachers of first-year university units each semester is the need to ensure that students learn, quickly, the methods and skills of correct referencing.[a] [In some courses, students are very much left to fend for themselves, relying on, perhaps, the services of the university library, advice offered by individual staff members, or simply muddling through on the basis of critical feedback on their first assignments.]**1** [The Department of Media and Information (DMI), along with some other areas of the university,[b] takes a different approach.]**2** [DMI, in its first-year unit MCI 101: Research and Presentation Project, directly addresses the need that students have to learn correct referencing techniques, devoting some weeks and an assignment to that task.[c]]**3** [Students can also practise these techniques in the assignments required in other first-year units.]**4**

This first paragraph establishes that it is reasonable to claim that DMI takes a different approach. It does so, in the premises, by claiming what other departments do, and then claims that what DMI does differs from this. Here are three interesting features of the paragraph:

a   The first sentence is not part of the argument directly. However, this sentence does contribute. When claim 2 says 'takes a different approach', the question that needs to be answered is 'a different approach to what?'. The first sentence provides the answer... 'a different approach to the problem...[etc].'

b   The phrase 'along with some other areas of the university' is not properly supported in the argument, as there is no evidence about these other areas. Technically, one might say, it is unproven.

c   The phrase 'devoting some weeks and an assignment to that task' might be thought by some to be a separate claim, embedded in claim 3. Possibly: but I would see it as detail which expands on and makes sensible the part of claim 3 that says 'directly addresses'—the detail shows how it is direct.

By way of example, here is the basic analytical structure that might be seen to lie beneath this narrative flow:

2.   *The Department of Media and Information takes a different approach to some other parts of Curtin University in solving the problem of ensuring that students in first-year university units each semester learn, quickly, the methods and skills of correct referencing.*

1.   *In some courses, students are very much left to fend for themselves, relying on, perhaps, the services of the university library, advice offered by individual staff members, or simply muddling through on the basis of critical feedback on their first assignments.*

3.   *The Department of Media and Information uses its first-year unit MCI 101: Research and Presentation Project to address directly the need that students have to learn the methods and skills of correct referencing by devoting some weeks in class and an assignment to that goal.*

4.   *Students in the Department of Media and Information also practise the methods and skills of correct referencing learned in MCI 101: Research and Presentation Project in the assignments required in other first-year units that they are studying at the same time.*

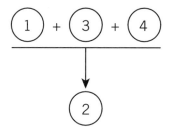

Moving on to the second paragraph:

[Nevertheless, even when direct attention of the kind[d] just outlined has been paid to referencing, some students continue to struggle with it.]**5** [The problem is not merely a technical one]**6**, since[e] [all the students at university are capable of learning to follow the kinds of technical directions that lay out the appropriate steps needed to reference their work.]**7** What then is the cause of this problem?[f] DMI would suggest that [many students (including some who are quite able referencers) remain confused about the admittedly complex set of reasons that explain *why* referencing is so important in all kinds of written communication.]**8** This paper will outline these reasons before ending with a short exploration of why they might be hard for some students to grasp.

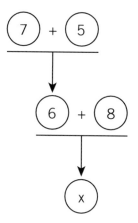

This paragraph is complex. For one thing, it does not have a clear conclusion. It is both 'structuring' the paper and also advancing an argument for that structure. I would imagine the implied conclusion, marked here as 'x', to be something like 'The cause of the problem is that students remain confused about these reasons'. There are also a number of assumptions made which mean there are implied premises. Here are three interesting features of the paragraph:

d. This inter-paragraph reference clearly demonstrates how the analytical structure cannot be easily read off 'the words in front of us', but depends on the surrounding narrative flow.

e. 'Since' tells us that, even though we might ourselves not imagine the claim following it is a premise for the claim that precedes it, we have no choice but to diagram it in this way. The author intends that we use the claim 7 as a premise for 6, and we diagram as the author intended.

f. This question is not a claim, but prompts us to think about the implied conclusion.

Here is the analytical structure of the first argument in this passage (what we can call a sub-argument because it is subsidiary to, but part of the overall argument in the paragraph), but this time making explicit the implied premise. See how 'obvious' it is?

5. *Nevertheless, some students continue to struggle with the methods and skills of correct referencing even when direct attention has been paid to learning it, as for example in MCI 101: Research and Presentation Project.*

7. *All students at university are capable of learning to follow the kinds of*

technical directions that lay out the appropriate steps needed to reference their work.

   i. *If everyone can follow the technical directions, then some people's failure to follow them indicates that technical matters are not the problem.*

   6. *The problem of some students struggling with the methods and skills of correct referencing is not merely a technical one.*

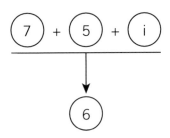

The third paragraph is not reasoning:

As just indicated, there are three main reasons why referencing is important in essays, reports, presentations, theses, articles, and all the other kinds of scholarly writing in which students engage both at university and then, as graduates, in their professions. Without seeking to assign a priority to any of them they are: first, that referencing enables a reader to seek out more information on the topic of the written work, based on the references given; second, referencing acknowledges authors' ethical and academic debt of thanks to those sources which they have used to create their own 'source' of information; and third, referencing provides a method by which authors can establish the validity and strength of their claims by relying on the authority of the source to which they are referring. Let us examine these reasons in more detail.

It identifies the three reasons and then says that the paper will examine them. Since there is no attempt to argue or explain why there are three reasons, or why the paper is looking at them in detail, and so on, there is nothing to be cast. Then, in paragraph 4:

[The process of effective scholarship (finding, analysing and communicating information) involves an almost-constant acquisition of ideas, knowledge, views, and general contextual understanding.]9 [One method of finding the material from which to acquire this information, used mainly at times of intensive research, is to follow the leads provided in an article or book via the references to find, quickly and with a high degree of reliability, additional valuable, relevant sources of information.]10 [A well-constructed piece of scholarly writing will contain both information in its own right and information that assists readers in further information acquisition.]11. Thus [an author needs to see referencing as a service to the reader of their work.]12 and, [using the kinds of standard methods that are available (such as the APA system)]**13**, make sure readers are easily able to go from their text to others via those references.]**14**.

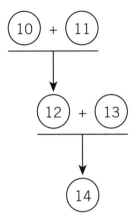

The last sentence could either contain two claims and an implied claim or three claims. Since the phrase starting 'using…' is what I use to infer the existence of the implied claim, I think it is best cast as three claims as indicated. Obviously the phrase 'using…' is not, in its current form, a complete claim. I would suggest that what it is really saying is: 'if referencing is a service to readers, then readers will only be able to benefit from this service by going to other texts via the references when an author uses the kinds of standard methods that are available'.

The second reason noted above was that[g] [authors owe a debt to those other writers who have provided them with information, inspiration and ideas.]**15** [This debt is both scholarly and ethical.]**16** What do I mean by assigning two different aspects to this notion of debt? Following the 'debt' metaphor through a little further, it is possible to say first that [the scholarly community within which an author writes enforces payment of the debt]**17** [(their readers will check their work, either consciously or not, for evidence that proper referencing has taken place)]**18**. Second, [it is enforced, or at least made possible, by the ethical behaviour of individual authors who, privately, must recognise they need to acknowledge those other writers who have helped them.]**19** [Without referencing, the system of mutual obligation on authors to use each others' work, to link new pieces of work to those already published, and to rely on one another's specific expertise would collapse.]**20** Thus [referencing is important, even if the references were never actually followed up[h] (though, of course, they regularly are).]**21**

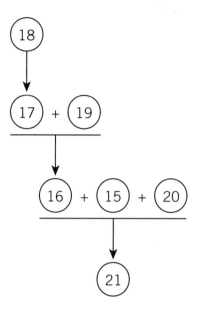

A difficult paragraph, not least because the ideas being presented are complex and metaphorical. A key feature here is to discern that there are sub-arguments within the main argument. That is, some of the reasoning here proves other claims that then help demonstrate the validity of conclusions further 'down' the chain of reasoning. As well, there is an important implied premise that links 16,15, and 20 together. Can you identify it? Here are two interesting features of the paragraph:

g. In both cases, the extra words here are not part of the claims which follow them. They help readers follow the narrative flow but are not, analytically, significant.

h. We have looked at how claims contain elements that indicate scope; normally we see these elements limiting the scope. However, in this case, the phrase 'even if…' extends the scope of the claim, attempting to counter any challenge to the logic by people who say 'ah, but references are not always checked'.

Moving on:

The third reason why referencing is so important is, perhaps, the most difficult to grasp. [References allow an author to obviate the need to detail and support every single premise in their arguments and explanations.]x by [relying instead on the authority of the source from which they obtained the information they are presenting.]y [(see Allen, *Smart Thinking*, chapter 6 for more explanation).]z Put simply, [references are part of the way one writes a convincing argument or explanation.]22 Since [good writing always seeks to be convincing, even if to only a small degree]23[i], then it is easy to see why[j] [the quest to teach students to be good writers must also involve teaching them to reference effectively.]24

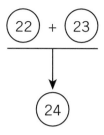

This paragraph contains repetition and the main analytical point being made does not start until claim 22. However, to be thorough, I have also demonstrated how the first part of the paragraph contains a 'side argument' (of sorts) (see below). Here are two interesting features of the paragraph:

i.   This claim is the *general rule* that is being applied to make the link from 22 to 24. Therefore this claim is the framing premise; and the type of reasoning in the whole 22, 23, and 24 ensemble is general-to-specific.

j.   The trace of reasoning 'then it is easy to see why' does *not* form part of the claim and is therefore excluded from the brackets.

Here's how the 'side argument' can be written out:

x.   References allow an author to obviate the need to detail and support every single premise in their arguments and explanations.

y.   References allow an author to rely on the authority of the source from which they obtained the information they are presenting.

a.   Relying on the authority of the source from which authors obtained the information they are presenting obviates the need to detail and support every single premise in their arguments and explanations.

z.   Allen, writing in *Smart Thinking*, chapter 6 explains the way in which references allow an author instead to rely on the authority of the source from which they obtained the information they are presenting in more detail.

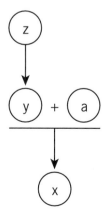

Note how the reference to *Smart Thinking* serves to support the claim **y**, thereby modelling the use of referencing which is the subject of the reason explained in the paragraph.

The next paragraph is not reasoning. It summarises the three previous paragraphs and their connection to the main theme.

> These three reasons can be summed up as follows. Each newly produced essay, article, presentation, or whatever, is always based substantially in existing published or presented material and becomes a part of the 'ongoing, knowledgeable conversation' expressed through that material. Written work needs good referencing so as to *refer* its readers elsewhere, to *repay* the debt to other writers, and to *reinforce* its own arguments.

However, the next paragraph is an argument:

> But what makes it hard for some students to grasp the essential elements of this relatively simple argument as to why they must reference, even as they dutifully follow out the instructions to 'reference correctly' laid out for them by teachers?[k] Without going into detail, it seems likely that [many students do not yet believe themselves to be authors, with an audience, and a comradeship with other authors. They see themselves primarily as students, governed by a debilitating and unequal regime of inequality in relation to their teachers.]**25** <u>Thus,</u> [the reasons I have just outlined are not rejected by some students because[l] they are not understood, or are unreasonably or wilfully ignored. Rather the reasons are rejected because they are, quite rationally, not relevant to a 'student', even if they are explained to students.]**26** [A 'student' (by which I mean the abstract identity rather than any particular individual) is governed by the imperatives of 'doing as one is told' by teachers;]**27** [a student's audience is their assessor;]**28** [a student's sense of comradeship is with other students as students;]**29** [the goal of writing is not, usually, 'contributing to human knowledge' but getting a good mark.]**30**

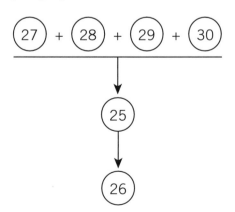

The most difficult paragraph in the text. First of all, the two sentences which I have combined as claim 26 might appear to be two claims. Since they are stating 'two sides of the coin', we might better represent them as one claim, even though the words are split over two sentences. Claim 25 shows a similar 'they are not—they are' pairing which is, effectively in this case, one claim.

What this example demonstrates is the lack of clarity of casting: it is an inexact science, in many cases depending on the way that a particular reader interprets the passage, rather than on all readers agreeing with a single interpretation. While we might use casting as an *exercise* to understand better analytical structure and logic, we should not confuse the exercise with practice. If the specific goal of the exercise of casting is to decide on the claims and their structure, its more general goal is to improve your understanding so that the 'real' goal—better critical thinking in your own writing—is more obtainable. Here are two interesting features:

k. I have indicated earlier in this book that questions can be thought of as 'claims-in-prospect' or, more fully, that a question is the way we propose a claim so as to then find the answers we need (the reasons) that will either support or reject that proposed claim. This question demonstrates the point. It says 'But what makes it hard for some students to grasp the essential elements of this relatively simple argument as to why they must reference, even as they dutifully follow out the instructions to 'reference correctly' laid out for them by teachers?', which in fact helps us to understand what the paragraph is attempting to do. It is not arguing that students do find it hard ... it is seeking to explore the reasons, the 'what makes it hard'.

l. Be careful! In this special case 'because' is part of the claim. The claim is claiming a link between the effect (ignoring referencing) and the cause (not failure to grasp, but failure to see them as relevant). Hence, in this case, because does not signal two separate claims.

The difficulty with the next paragraph (and, indeed, the previous one) is that it relies on many assumptions and already-established ideas from the rest of the text. Moreover, the paragraph combines explanation (explaining why something happens) and argument, in that it argues for one explanation over another.

[Students in general then fail to understand the need to reference.]**32** because [they do not see how the very sensible arguments in favour of referencing apply to them]**33**. <u>Thus</u>, in terms of the cultural understanding of student identity—of 'who students believe themselves to be'—<u>we can see that</u> [students probably fail to reference effectively because they are not motivated by genuine self-interest as writers, but instead by the dubious and failure-prone motivation of obedience.]**34**

The last paragraph is a summary of what comes before and I have not cast it.

Capturing the essence of the text

Looking back over the last three paragraphs, I have tried to produce something of the key argument they contain as a list of claims and diagram. In doing so, I hope not only to assist you in understanding the text as a whole but also to show how casting is not 'the only way of doing things'. Sometimes we can try to understand things by reconstructing the underlying argument structure, rather than directly recovering it from the narrative flow. I have changed the words, and stripped the argument down to its essentials so as to make clear what the logic is. This is not casting. I am doing it here simply to show you another use for the methods of thinking about logic I have discussed in this book.

1. We need to make students think of themselves as writers and not as students.
2. Students write for an assessor.
3. Students have comradeship with other students.
4. Students write with the goal of getting a good mark.
5. Students write as a result of being told to write.
6. Being a writer means believing that the goal of writing is contributing to knowledge.
7. Being a writer means thinking of one's audience as those people with something to learn from the writer.
8. Being a writer means having a sense of comradeship with other authors.
9. Being a writer means writing with self-motivation to write.
10. Students do not write as if they are writers, but write as students.
11. Referencing only seems relevant if one is a writer.
12. Students know technically how to reference.

13. The most likely explanation of students' failures to reference is that they do not think of themselves as writers.
14. We do not want students to fail to reference.

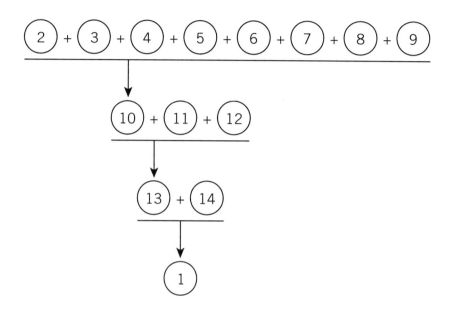

Overall narrative flow of the text

There are ten paragraphs in the text. Here is what each of them does, as part of a narrative flow that expresses the underlying logical structure:

1   Sets the scene by providing background information and grabbing the reader's attention by establishing that there is a problem that needs to be considered.

2   This paragraph provides crucial signalling information about the whole piece. It identifies that there is something interesting about the solution proposed by it to the problem (always useful to know when one is looking for new and different ideas), and signals that the paper has a two-part structure.

3   A further set of signals about the organisation of the paper. It identifies that there will be three reasons, and each will be examined in detail.

4,5,6 Each of these paragraphs covers one of the three reasons signalled in paragraph 3. This structure shows how paragraphing can help, indirectly, to sustain the argument … reflecting the intellectual decisions about what and how many reasons in the words on the page.

7   Sums up these reasons in an accessible way. It is not a conclusion. It summarises. Paragraphs like this are useful to help readers grasp what has been communicated since reading something twice helps to embed it in their minds.

8   Commences the second part of the text, as cued by the question and by the fact that the preceding paragraph was a summary.

9   Continues the second part, stating the main conclusion for this part of the paper.

10   Takes the material from paragraphs 8 and 9 and relates it back to the problem and context with which the text commenced in paragraphs 1 and 2. It briefly mentions the material from paragraphs 3 to 7 so as to make a comprehensive endpoint.

Summary

This book has concentrated on the analytical structure format, primarily as a way of learning about reasoning, but also with an eye to its practical application as a tool for helping you plan the creation and presentation of arguments and explanations. Yet it would be wrong to think that the format is, of itself, something essential to reasoning. It is not. This format—along with the idea of analytical questions—is one way of representing the thought processes that we must go through to be smart thinkers. It enables us to see that the key elements of smart thinking are:

- being thoughtful in considering issues in depth and with breadth, and without 'missing' any element of reasoning
- being critical in the way we assess information, not taking things for granted or making easy assumptions, either about the truth of claims or their inter-relationships with other claims
- being smart in the way we relate the texts of reasoning to the contexts in which they are produced, presented, and then used
- being aware that 'knowledge' and 'reasoning' represent two perspectives on the same fundamental concept: that we explain and argue about the world in terms of the links between objects and ideas. No one idea or object can be understood except in relation to others.

Smart thinking is not just a method or skill. It is also an attitude. Practising and using the skills, with a clear awareness of what you are doing and a willingness to reflect on and learn about the process of reasoning, will give you the right approach to being a smart thinker, effective in your reasoning and able to achieve your goals through arguments and explanations. Good luck!

Answers, Discussion, and Further Advice

Chapter 1
Exercise 1.1

Asking questions (of ourselves and others). Your questions are designed to tell you what you do not already know and guide you in what to find out; but they also draw out hidden aspects of a problem; and, because questions are like claims (see chapter 2), they provide possible conclusions for your argument. You will find that questions are essential to good reasoning, and in chapter 9 we focus on the questions you need to ask.

Seek out information. Smart thinking requires information. It also helps us when dealing with information by letting us sift through for the essential things we want to know. Chapter 8 provides guidance on how to search for and recover information analytically—that is, as part of the reasoning process.

Make connections. This activity is crucial. If you are not doing this, you are not thinking smart. It is like doing a jigsaw puzzle—if you put the pieces together in the right way, you come up with the 'right answer' (the picture) at the end. The connections we might make between separate pieces of evidence or ideas are demonstrated most clearly in chapters 3 and 4.

Interpret and evaluate. Not only do you need to interpret and evaluate what you read: you also need to do these actions to your own thinking! Chapters 5 and 6 are all about improving your reasoning and in that process evaluation is critical.

Exercise 1.2

Questioning is rather like concept- or mind-mapping (see chapter 9). However, it is important that you treat this exercise as one of asking (not trying to answer) the questions. Too often we begin to answer a question or two that concern us without having first thought about what other questions need asking.

Chapter 2

Exercise 2.1

Statements **b**, **e**, and **f** are claims.

Exercise 2.2

a   two claims: 'All that glitters is gold'; 'this nugget glitters'.
b   one claim: 'The song is called "Diamonds are a Girl's Best Friend"', concealed in a rhetorical question.
c   three claims: 'Silver jewellery is very common'; 'silver is a cheap metal', 'it [silver] is easily worked'. Note the use of the pronoun 'it'.

Exercise 2.3

a   'Drinking milk' *subject* makes 'some people feel sick' *predicate*
b   'I' *subject* 'do not drink milk' *predicate*
c   'Milk drinking' *subject* is 'not recommended for people who are lactose-intolerant' *predicate*

Exercise 2.4

a   'drinking milk makes some people feel sick'. This direct claim has been made by the doctor. The actual meaning of the entire claim is that I have been told this claim.
b   'I drink milk' 'I feel sick'. There are two claims here, effectively, combined to make a propositional super-claim.
c   'a person comes to a doctor and says "If I drink milk, then I feel sick"' and 'the doctor will diagnose that person as lactose-intolerant'. These are the two claims in the if/then statement; note also that the first claim is itself an indirect claim, like (a).

Exercise 2.5

Order of scope: **b**, **a**, **c**. The key words are (**b**) 'Whenever', (**a**) 'Sometimes', and (**c**) 'Occasionally'. Order of certainty: **e**, **d**, **f**. The key words are (**e**) 'There is no way', (**d**) 'probable', and (**f**) 'the odds are 50:50'. The linkages are between (**a**) milk-drinking and sickness; (**b**) eating cheese before sleeping and dreams; (**c**) eating rich food and indigestion; and (**d–f**) humans and living in space.

Exercise 2.6

Claims **a** and **c** are explicit value claims; claim **b** has an implied value judgment; claim **d** is (probably) simply descriptive. Where is the value judgment in claim **b**? It does, of course, depend on context, but most people in contemporary Australia recognise that 'fat is bad for you'. Hence, claiming that some product contains fat connects it with this value judgment; equally, though, there are some situations in which fat is good for you (or at least better than avoiding it altogether). On the other hand, is there some value judgment in claim **d**? In certain contexts, the idea that 'white is pure' (and hence 'good for you') could be implied by this claim, thus making it, to some extent, a value judgment. If you found this exercise hard, you have done well: judging and identifying value claims depends, by and large, on the contexts in which we find those claims.

Exercise 2.7

Some examples: 'Because the road is wet [p], you need to drive more carefully [c]'; 'Because you need to drive more carefully [p], you should pay attention to what you are doing [c]'; 'I conclude that there was a rainstorm a few minutes ago [c] because Verity has just come home soaking wet [p]'; 'There was a rainstorm a few minutes ago [p] and so the road is wet [c]'. In preparation for chapter 3, think about the role of words such as 'because', 'I conclude', and so on.

Exercise 2.8

Conclusions **a** and **d** are appeals to action, with the latter involving a change in thinking. Note the disguised claim in the rhetorical question. Conclusion **b** makes a prediction. Conclusion **c** is an explanation showing how the conclusion comes about. Conclusion **e** is a justification on the part of the government for its past actions (as stated in the conclusion).

Chapter 3

Exercise 3.1

Some examples of the way to rewrite them are:
a   I was elated because, today, I found out that I had passed my exam. (Two claims now contained in one sentence.)
b   I felt ill and so I went home from work. (Still two claims in one sentence but different way of signalling the conclusion... 'so'.)
c   Thinking helps us to do better at work; and thinking improves our performance at university. So we better learn to do it! (Changing where the nouns and pronouns fit, and the order.)

d   John is a fully qualified lawyer because he passed his final exams. (Change of order.)

e   Many tourists come to Australia because Australia has great natural beauty and a marvellous climate. (Change of order.)

Exercise 3.2

Here are two possible answers, with the linking words in italics.

1   You should drive more carefully *because of the fact that* wet roads increase the risk of accident and the road is *indeed* wet. [The word 'indeed' may or may not be some sort of signal that this claim is a premise linked to the conclusion; it suggests that the truth of the claim 'the road is wet' is very obvious. In reasoning we use better known or accepted claims as the premises to prove a less obvious one.]

2   *Can you not see that* you should drive more carefully? I mean the road is wet and *we know that* wet roads increase the risk of accident. [The conclusion has been expressed as a rhetorical question; as a standard claim, it would read '*You must see that* you should drive more carefully'.]

Exercise 3.3

The order of the claims in the structure is more logical, especially when cross-referenced to the diagram, which shows the sequence of arguments. The claims are written without pronouns, so each is meaningful in and of itself. The arrows and other symbols in the diagram show the specific links between claims, rather than being hidden in the narrative flow. The claims in the analytical structure are self-contained: you don't need to read any other claim to know what each means whereas in the narrative flow, you do.

Exercise 3.4

a   (I should not buy a car at the moment) **1**. (I have just lost my driver's licence) **2** and, besides, (I cannot afford it) **3**.

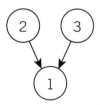

There are no link words that might signal the conclusion or premises. However, of the three claims, claim 1 is the obvious conclusion. If claims 2 or 3 were the conclusion, then the argument would make very little, if any, sense at all. In this case, the premises do not add together. While the word 'and' might suggest they do, either premise on its own would be sufficient to support the conclusion. Hence they are independent of one another in the diagram. (See chapter 4.)

b　(Nicole Kidman is an international movie star) **1** and <u>I know that</u>, (as a general rule, international movie stars get paid a lot of money) **2**. <u>Therefore, it is obvious that</u> (Nicole Kidman is well paid) **3**.

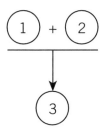

This example should be easier than the first. This time there are two linking phrases, which clearly show the conclusion and one of the premises. Claims 1 and 2 are dependent on one another, meaning they must be 'grouped' together. (See chapter 4.)

c　(I have not got a university education, whereas several of my colleagues do) **1**. (All of them have recently received promotions, but I did not receive one) **2**. <u>Given that</u> (we are all roughly equal in our job performance) **3**, <u>I would have to conclude that</u> (a university education really helps one to get ahead in a career) **4**.

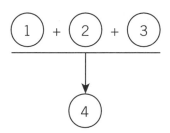

It is equally acceptable to separate claims 1 and 2 into four claims (that is, 'I have not got a university education' as the first, 'several of my colleagues do [have a university education]' as the second, and so on), but it does not clarify the analytical structure. The trick here is to avoid being fooled by the punctuation: the first three claims are all dependent premises, despite being spread over three sentences and despite the lack of clear signals for the first two claims. See the section 'Special function of premises' in chapter 4 for a discussion of how one claim

(claim 3 in this example) plays a significant role in explaining why the other premises lead to a particular conclusion.

d   <u>What was the explanation for</u> (Sydney beating Beijing for the 2000 Olympics) **1**? <u>There were two main reasons.</u> (The Sydney organisers did a better job of lobbying the International Olympic Committee delegates) **2** and, <u>because of</u> (political crises in China at the time) **3** and (perceived doubts about Beijing's quality of services and venues) **4**, (Sydney offered a much safer venue for a successful Olympic games) **5**.

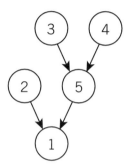

This example is the hardest. The 'two main reasons' signal might confuse you about the nature of claims 3 and 4. But think about what the author is trying to say with the 'because'. It does not relate to claim 1, but gives two reasons for claim 5. We can think of these last three claims as a sub-argument. Claim 5 functions as the conclusion in this sub-argument but then becomes a premise in the main explanation. Note, too, that 'political crises in China' is a short-hand way of saying 'There were political crises in China at that time', and similarly for claim 4. Read further in chapter 3 for a discussion of the role of these sub-arguments inside a main argument or explanation.

Exercise 3.5

First, do not write, as if it were one claim, a statement that is either not a claim or is two claims. For example, the sentence 'We should study reasoning because it will help us to understand our world better' contains two claims, linked with the word 'because'. For your analytical structure to be workable, each numbered statement must be one claim only. Use your analytical structure diagram to show the relationship signalled by words such as 'because'. Labelling 'Reasoning is that skill that' as claim 1 and 'helps us to solve problems' as claim 2 is also wrong. One claim has, in this example, been split falsely into two non-claims. A claim needs to connect internally *two* key ideas or concepts. 'Reasoning is that skill that helps us to solve problems' is *one* claim, connecting reasoning with the idea of solving problems.

Second, do not write claims that make no sense on their own. While narrative writing and speaking requires the use of pronouns and other short-hand phrases, for planning purposes we should write more precisely. The following example, for instance, is incorrect:

1   Matthew Allen is the author of a book on reasoning.
2   He works at Curtin University.
3   This is a short, practically oriented book.

Using 'he' and 'this' are confusing. You need to use the appropriate nouns, as in the following example:

1   Matthew Allen is the author of a book on reasoning.
2   Matthew Allen works at Curtin University.
3   The book on reasoning that Matthew Allen wrote is short and practically oriented.

Third, avoid mistakes in diagramming the interrelationship of claims. Some mistakes in this area are the result of not understanding clearly what you want to say—later chapters will help you to overcome these mistakes. Other mistakes result from not grasping the meaning of the diagram symbols. Here are two examples. First of all, imagine I had argued that:

1   Reasoning skills should be taught more in Australian schools [as my conclusion].
2   Reasoning is a key skill which all people should know about [as my premise].

It would be *incorrect* to diagram their relationship thus:

Although I have *written* the conclusion first, the only place for a conclusion in the diagram is *below* the premise(s) that support it. The [↓] symbol indicates a logical relationship (in this case, 'because 2, therefore 1') and not the order in which you would write or say these claims.

Now imagine my argument was more complex:

1   Reasoning skills should be taught more in Australian schools.
2   Reasoning is a key skill which all people should know about.
3   Schools should teach people the key skills which they need.

It would be *incorrect* to diagram their relationship thus:

Claims 2 and 3 are related and, indeed, are dependent on one another (see chapter 4). It is wrong to use the [↓] symbol for any form of relationship between claims other than for the logical relationship 'because ... therefore'. Instead the + symbol should have been used to join claims 2 and 3 on the same line.

Other *incorrect* uses of the diagram tend to reflect a misunderstanding of the fact that, first, the diagramming process must reflect what is written in the text (i.e. the diagram brings out, explicitly, the relationships between premises and conclusions implicit in the wording of those claims); and second, a simple misunderstanding that the line, arrow, and plus symbols must be used very precisely, to mean only one thing. Here are examples of technical mistakes in diagramming you need to avoid:

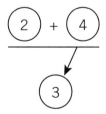

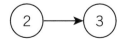

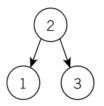

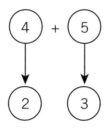

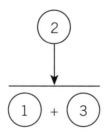

Exercise 3.6

[The current Australian government is, in many ways, challenging the role of the United Nations as a body that promotes action by member nations to maintain and extend human rights within those nations' own jurisdiction.]1 [This challenge has a distinct and dangerous consequence for Australia]2 (quite apart from arguments about its dubious morality) <u>because</u> [the challenge puts Australia in conflict with most other nations of the world over human rights]3 and [Australian trade and foreign relations are likely to suffer in the long run.]4 By definition, [this long-run result is dangerous.]5 <u>I believe that</u> [the government's role should be to work to avoid danger]6 <u>and, therefore, I believe</u> [the government's current approach to the UN over human rights is incorrect.]7

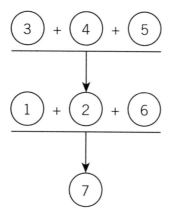

Claim 1

The subject is: 'The current Australian government is'

The predicate is: 'challenging the role of the United Nations as a body that promotes action by member nations to maintain and extend human rights within those nations' own jurisdiction'

Note the limitation on scope, '*in many ways*'.

Claim 2

The phrase in parentheses could be included in the claim; my answer excludes it because the words '*quite apart from...*' imply that there are other issues here that are not being discussed. Therefore it is not part of the overall logical structure. However, one could also read it as a limitation, of sorts, on the scope of claim 2, within this argument.

The subject is: 'This challenge' (note '*this*', linking back to the predicate of claim 1)

The predicate is: 'has a distinct and dangerous consequence for Australia'

Claim 3

The subject is: 'the challenge puts'

The predicate is: 'Australia in conflict with most other nations of the world over human rights'

Claim 4

This claim is a 'contracted' claim. What it really says is 'if Australia is in conflict with most other nations of the world over human rights, then Australian trade and foreign relations are likely to suffer in the long run'. One can see how the predicate of claim 3 is positioned as the first part of the 'if/then' claim, allowing the consequence of the challenge (the damage to trade and foreign relations) to be established.

The subject is: 'if Australia is in conflict with most other nations of the world over human rights'

The predicate is: 'then Australian trade and foreign relations are likely to suffer in the long run'

Claim 5

'*By definition*' could be included in this claim or not: it is, in some ways, a certainty element. It is saying 'definitely'. Alternatively, as I have done, it can be excluded as simply indicating the kind of claim being made (definitional).

The subject is: 'this long-term result'

The predicate is: 'is dangerous' (Note the way this clearly links to the predicate in the sub-conclusion, claim 2.)

Claim 6

'*I believe*' should be excluded here (though it does not really matter if you included it). If one is arguing, then it is taken that the claims on which you rely are those one believes. However, had the claim been about another person's beliefs, the correct answer would have included those words. The importance of claim 5, which first raised 'danger' and then the way 'danger' is included in claim 2 starts to become clear here.

The subject is: 'the government's role'

The predicate is: 'should be to work to avoid danger'

Claim 7

'*I believe*' can again be excluded here. If one is arguing, then it is taken for granted that the claims on which you rely are those you believe. However, had the claim been about another person's beliefs, the correct answer would have included those words. The subject of this claim is more detailed, so as to remind readers of the very first claim made.

The subject is: 'the government's current approach to the UN over human rights'

The predicate is: 'is incorrect'

The first part of the argument (3+4+5 → 2)

Claim 2 is presented 'because' ... and then some more claims. As a result, these claims are functioning as the premises for 2. Claim 2, therefore, functions as a conclusion to 3, 4, and 5 and then as a premise in the rest of the argument. Note the use of a proposition here (claim 4). 'If x happens, then y happens; x is happening; therefore y will happen'.

The second part of the argument (1+2+6 → 7)

Generally governments should work to avoid danger, the arguer is saying. In this specific case the government is not doing that. Therefore the government is wrong in this specific case.

Chapter 4

Exercise 4.1

Here is one possible answer. I have marked the main elements of interconnection with letters.

1   Australia should [a] continue to spend a proportion of its national budget on foreign aid [b].
2   Australia is morally obligated [c] to provide foreign aid [b].
3   If a nation is morally obligated to act [c], then it should [a].

Exercise 4.2

Here is one possible answer. Each premise functions as a different reason for the conclusion (one concerns economics and the other morality), unlike the previous exercise, in which two premises worked together to provide just one reason.

1   Australia should continue to spend a proportion of its national budget on foreign aid.
2   Providing economic aid is a prudent economic investment.
3   Australia is morally obligated to provide foreign aid.

Exercise 4.3

a   If one is sick, then one should not come to work.
b   When someone abuses your trust, they should be punished [another way of saying 'if someone abuses your trust, then they should be punished'].
c   All human life is worth protecting.

  In each case, notice how these premises tell us why the particular evidence given leads us to the stated conclusion. On that basis, here are the missing framework premises for the answers to exercise 4.2:

  1   Claim 2 needs claim 4: 'All nations should make prudent economic investments' (alternatively, 'if an action is economically prudent, then it should be pursued').
  2   Claim 3 needs claim 5: 'A nation should act on its moral obligations' (alternatively, 'if a nation has moral obligations, then it should act upon them').

  And the diagram for these claims is:

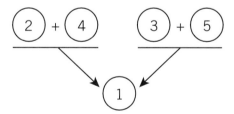

Exercise 4.4

Here are four definitions. Which example relates to which method?
a   Studying critical thinking is like learning to play a difficult sport well: you have to break it down into its components and practise each one.
b   By 'studying critical thinking' I mean learning to use reasoning for arguing and explaining and then learning about the context in which reasoning occurs.

c   Studying critical thinking is not the same as studying moral reasoning.

d   Studying critical thinking means, for example, reading a book like this one.

Exercise 4.5

The first argument is 2+3 → 4. Claims 2 and 4 are identical, except that 'assault' is replaced with 'threaten to attack'. Claim 3 does the work of making this equivalence. It might seem foolish but it is an important point: you do not actually have to touch someone to be charged with assault—the threat is sufficient. In this case, one might assume the audience did not know this point and the arguer was making it clear to them.

The second argument is 5 → 6. In a way claim 5 is actually saying a very similar thing to claim 6. However 5 relates to a specific survey; 6 concludes a general position on the basis of that survey. For example, the link is made in the consistency between 5 and 6; 150 out of 200 becomes the generalisation 'most' (which is reasonable).

The third argument is 8+9+10 → 11. This is a very good example of a framing premise (which in fact is concerned with establishing the causal relationship—see chapter 7). Claim 10 ensures that the change in state reported in 8 and 9 does therefore support 11. Note how, in 9, it is not saying the assault caused... (which would be circular), rather, it is simply identifying a time period in which Michael became depressed. The causal chain is asserted in the conclusion, 11.

The fourth argument is 4+6 → 7. Michael is the predicate of claim 4, but becomes the subject of claim 7 because 'victims' in claim 6 is a category to which Michael belongs.

The fifth argument is 7+12+13+11 → 1. Note how super-claim 12 contains something very similar to the claim 11 in the 'if' position, and that the conclusion 1 looks very similar to the 'then' sub-claim in 12. This would be sufficient on its own, except that the conclusion provides a specific time of imprisonment and thus claim 7 does the work of supporting that part of the concluding claim. Had you not included 7, it would be hard to argue why three to six months and not (say) a year or a day!

Chapter 5
Exercise 5.1

a   **Some years ago, the Northern Territory passed legislation allowing some people to commit voluntary euthanasia.**

There is no explicit value judgment. The claim is only about the Northern Territory, and some time ago, so in that respect, its scope is limited. The claim also reports the limited scope of the legislation itself: 'some people'. Implicitly, this claim is certain that the legislation was passed. Voluntary euthanasia sounds more clinical than, say, 'kill themselves'; while it might appear to be a more neutral term, in fact it probably connotes some sense that the act is more legitimate. This example should alert us to the value judgments concealed within attempts to be value-free.

b   **Most religious leaders at the time, and now, claim that legislation permitting voluntary euthanasia is immoral.**

This statement proposes simply that religious leaders have *claimed* the legislation to be immoral. As a result the claim itself (as it stands) is not necessarily making a value judgment. However, we would have to look at the way it is used in an argument or explanation. The scope is defined by the word 'most', with the claim also reporting the certainty of the 'original' claim—that the legislation is immoral—which implies a 100 per cent certainty. This claim (which is indirect) is certain of itself. The connotation that most springs to mind is that of 'leaders': while it certainly denotes particular people in church power structures, it perhaps connotes some sense that we should agree with these people (they are leaders and we should follow).

c   **If a state government passed voluntary euthanasia laws, then the Federal Government would not be able to stop that legislation in the same way that it did for the Northern Territory.**

This is an 'if . . . then' statement, with a connection between a cause ('if . . . ') and a predicted outcome of that cause (' . . . then'). Once again, there is no obvious value judgment, but we would have to look at the way in which it is used in the argument or explanation as a whole before being sure. This claim has been carefully constructed with due regard for scope and certainty: note the importance of 'similar' in the first half of the claim; then consider how the word 'likely' helps to reduce further the claim's ambit. The claim does not express a certain, but merely a likely, consequence.

d   **Several terminally ill people were reported in the media at the time as saying they were moving to the Northern Territory.**

As with claim **b**, the claim is about some other person's claim. As such, it may or may not imply a positive value judgment in favour of the euthanasia legislation, depending on the context. 'Several', in the first half of the claim, helps to define the scope. Whether or not the people do move may be uncertain (since they may not actually have done it, how can we be sure if they will), but the claim is itself expressed in a certain manner—they have certainly *told* the media making the claim of their intention.

e   **I imagine that if another state or territory were to pass similar laws, then media reporting of the legislation would be very extensive.**

This is, deliberately, a trick question. It is an if/then claim again. Remember that the 'I' who imagines is also the 'I' making this claim. It would be wrong to interpret it as a claim about what the person has imagined; rather, the phrase 'I imagine that' is a limitation on the certainty of the claim: the person making this claim really does not know for sure whether or not media reporting will be very extensive and uses that phrase to tell us so. The scope, on the other hand, is quite broad: media implies television, radio, and newspaper. Well-formed claims do not use confusing phrases like 'I imagine that'. Media reporting may well have considerable connotative aspects, depending on who was reading the claim.

f   **Some politicians argued that media reporting at the time of the Northern Territory legislation encouraged some terminally ill people to move there.**

An indirect descriptive claim with no real connotations (which are however very evident in the original claim).

Exercise 5.2

Generally speaking, I would judge that claims **b**, **e**, and **f** would be 'self-evident' to a general adult audience. They would, in effect, provide or hint at their own argument for foundation. Claim **d** is *not* self-evident because it is an explicit value claim. Few, if any, value claims can ever be safely regarded as self-evident because there are so many competing value systems at work in the world (and within Australia). Claims **a** and **c** involve strong implied values that would, among some members of the Australian population, create sufficient doubt for the claims not to be self-evident. Finally, the main reason for regarding a single claim to be self-evident is that all opposing claims are already disproved and/or the general knowledge of the broad community is good enough to provide a convincing argument for the claim, as, for example, in claim **f**.

If the idea of a 'general adult audience' posed problems for you, then that's good! Reflect on the need to have a well-developed understanding of which claims may or may not be regarded as self-evident.

Exercise 5.3

To support claim **a**, we could try a scholarly work on recent political history; alternatively, members of a communist (or ex-communist) country might provide support from their experience. Personal memories might be relevant authority for claim **b**; other good sources of authority would be a history book or, to be precise, the government legislation enacted in that year that authorised the introduction of television (see chapter 8 on direct sources). Claim **c** would, again, draw upon historical or political books for authority. Claim **d** is probably too contentious for an authority to be widely available or accepted. Perhaps we could use a report by social, medical, or legal experts. Claim **e**, on the other hand, could again be sourced from a political or history book. Note, however, possible disagreements about the term 'main'. A doctor or a medical textbook would be two sources of authority for claim **f**.

Exercise 5.4

a   An argument to support this claim would have to address the meaning of the word 'failed': Has communism failed communists or has it failed as a political and economic system? Does it mean failed of its own accord or defeated by the economic power of capitalism?

b   The strongly descriptive nature of this claim probably means that using authorities is better than using supporting reasoning for such a claim.

c   Although the Australian political system could be used as evidence, such an argument might not address the hidden implications that democracy here refers to the daily lives of Australia's citizens (freedom, choice, individuality) rather than the strict legal definition of the Australian political system.

d   The extreme nature of this claim (relative to majority opinion) would suggest the need for a strong supporting argument that might explain the benefits to society (if any) of such a step.

e   This is a descriptive claim; it would be better to leave it as self-evident in case our readers become incensed that we feel the need to convince them of something so 'obvious'!

f   We might recognise situations in which, even with a broken leg, immediate medical treatment is impossible or inappropriate. Any argument would have to take such considerations into account.

Note my advice that claims **b** and **f** do not require argument but, instead, reference to authority. Deciding when not to reason directly for a claim is part of the smart thinker's bag of tricks. Generally speaking, these six claims need to be assessed, first of all, in relation to the events, situations, or decisions that they represent. Such an assessment is the traditional objective judgment of truth: if the 'objects' described or stated in the claim are truly represented, then the claims are acceptable. But, it is not enough to assess in this manner when thinking about communicating an argument or explanation. Reasoning is a social act, which requires us to think about the contexts in which we might provide arguments and explanations: what do *others* judge these claims to be? We must reason in ways that take account of the knowledge and assumptions of our audience, and also conform to the accepted conventions of the circumstances in which we are arguing or explaining. For example, an audience of marijuana-smokers may well accept claim **d** without question; an audience of young people who have 'always' had television in their lives might need the support of some authority before accepting claim **b**; in an academic paper or essay, claim **e**, obvious though it may be, would need to be given some explanation and analysis; in a short discussion between paramedics at a motor vehicle crash, claim **f** would probably be stated without the need for argument in its favour. Finally, decisions about the extent to which we present claims as being self-evident depend on our conclusions. In any argument or explanation, it is the specific conclusion that can help us determine (given the inevitable limitations on available time or space for reasoning) what we explain in more detail and what we leave for the audience to accept or reject on their own. (See chapter 9.)

Chapter 6
Exercise 6.1

For conclusion **a**, one reason might be 'I want to improve my reasoning skills'. To unpack this reason requires that you consider *why* reading a book on critical thinking would help you to do this. In doing so, you address each of the issues raised by the conclusion. For example (in the form 2+3+4 → 1):

1. I am reading a book on reasoning.
2. I want to improve my reasoning skills.
3. I cannot improve my reasoning skills without knowing more about reasoning.
4. A book is an excellent source of knowledge about reasoning.

For conclusion **b**, an initial reason might be that 'thinking better stops you from being tricked by clever advertising'. See how many different issues are involved that are quite distinct from the conclusion? Each must be covered in some way in the premises, for example (in the form 2+3+4+5 → 1):

1. There are considerable benefits to be gained from studying how to think better.
2. I do not want to be tricked by clever advertising.
3. Clever advertising works by tricking you into buying products.
4. Thinking clearly stops you being tricked by clever advertising.
5. Studying how to think better does enable you to think clearly.

Exercise 6.2

a   The premise 'there were many people waiting at the station' is irrelevant. While trains crash for a variety of reasons (human error, sabotage, faulty machinery, and so on), the number of people waiting at a station is rarely, if ever, a cause of the crash. Even if the claim is true, it adds no greater explanation to why the train crashed and thus is irrelevant.

b   There are no irrelevant premises here. The second premise, concerning competition, might seem to be irrelevant (given that the conclusion is about privatisation); however, the first premise, with its connection between competition and privatisation, makes it relevant.

c   The premise 'politicians get too many benefits' is irrelevant (since there are no further premises to make it relevant to the conclusion). Whether or not it is true does nothing to make the conclusion more likely to be accepted. Now, we may well wonder if there is another irrelevant premise. However, the conclusion as stated involves two elements: a question of trust (and whether or not politicians lie obviously bears on this question) and a question of the quality of their decisions (and politicians' knowledge is relevant to this matter). Relevance is specifically concerned with the relationship between premise and conclusion.

Exercise 6.3

For each of the four conclusions, here are one relevant and one irrelevant premise (can you see which is which?):

a   'In a democracy, voting is not just a right but a civic duty' and 'Many European swallows fly south for the winter'.

b   'Humans can only survive if the environment is well protected' and 'Mining activities in Australia usually trespass on Aboriginal lands'.

c   'Eighty per cent of the songs on commercial radio come from the USA' and 'My family watches *The Simpsons* every night'.

d   'Personal computers help us to work, study, and relax' and 'There are two main types of personal computer: the PC and the Macintosh'.

The *first premise*, in each case, is relevant. Note how *all of* the premises are acceptable, even though in some cases they are patently irrelevant (as in exercise 6.3 (a)).

The most important questions to ask yourself after doing this exercise are: Why do some irrelevant premises *appear* relevant? What mistakes do we make when we misjudge relevance? Reflect on these questions and come up with some answers in relation to an area of knowledge or expertise with which you are familiar.

Exercise 6.4

Looking back to exercise 6.3, I would add the following claims to the premises given above:

a   If something is a duty, then it is acceptable for it to be compulsory.

b   Economic development is pointless if humans do not survive.

c   American songs are culturally loaded with American values and opinions.

d   The help given by a personal computer is only available if you actually own a personal computer.

Can you see here how errors in relevance are usually associated with picking the wrong dependent framework premise? When we think that a premise is relevant to a conclusion and, on reflection, we decide that it is not, usually we are changing our minds about the framework premise that goes along with it.

Try changing the four premises given in these answers. If you change them enough, can you make the original four premises from exercise 6.3 irrelevant? For instance, in example **a**, if the framework premise was 'Not all duties should be compulsory', the original premise ('In a democracy, voting is not just a right but a civic duty') does not become 'false' (it remains acceptable), but it simply is not relevant to the specific conclusion 'Voting at elections should be compulsory'.

Exercise 6.5

Claim 2 requires a claim such as 'We should understand what is happening now'. In the context of a class of first-year university students (caught up in their own concerns, and finding and discovering themselves at university), I would probably explicitly establish this relevance, allowing me to argue for the truth of this additional framing premise (which is in itself doubtful for these students, in my experience) and also to show clearly the relevance of the first premise. I would not, however, make such an explicit argument for an audience of academics who themselves study the contemporary world.

Claim 3 requires a claim such as 'Stories of the fight for democracy and justice in the past can help us to maintain and improve democracy and justice in the present' (which, one assumes, is what we want to do). In the context of writing an article for a readership of left-wing historians, for example (a group whose professional life involves precisely the activity that this premise describes), I would *not* include this claim explicitly. For non-historians, however, I would explicitly include it to make my argument clear.

Claim 4 requires a claim such as 'It is important to learn how to write essays'. Professional historical researchers, although they know much about history and, on reflection, would accept this new claim, would not, in my experience, immediately see *the relevance of* claim 4 to the conclusion and would thus need the additional claim to make the relevance explicit. In the context of talking to high-school history teachers, however, I would probably not include it explicitly.

Exercise 6.6

Context basically involves *both* audiences and knowledge. In a sense, we know and think about audiences in terms of what they know and what they expect *us* to know. We know that reasoning is about linking claims together in various ways. We will do this in our own reasoning, but when our audience hears or reads it, they will themselves immediately 'connect' what we have presented to their existing knowledge. If they know something that we have *not* included and make connections that run counter to our general argument, then we will fail to convince them. If, at the moment, you are studying or working and must regularly produce reasoning in some form, reflect on any stated, explicit requirements that you must meet in this presentation. Try to determine what underlying assumptions about reasoning these requirements express. (See also chapters 8 and 9.)

Exercise 6.7

a   The scope and certainty involved make it a strong conclusion. However, the particular burden of proof involved in proving this conclusion would be affected by the audience and by its existing commitments to, and understanding of, the claim. Serving military officers, for whom national service involves considerable disruption to their preferred volunteer armed forces, would need more convincing than, say, a conservative group of older veterans who themselves had undertaken national service.

b   Words like 'one option' and 'some' limit the scope considerably and make it a mild conclusion. Yet the burden of proof involved in proving this claim to a group of peace activists, for whom military service would *never* be an appropriate option, would still be very high.

c   This is tricky because the claim is stated with certainty but is of fairly limited scope (not advocating service, but an inquiry). Moreover, the word 'possibility' suggests that the inquiry may not conclude that military service should be introduced. It is strong, but only in the precise context of the establishment of an inquiry. Note that, from the perspective of someone who has already made up their mind that national service should be introduced, a commitment to establishing an inquiry will seem like an opposing conclusion, especially in a context in which it is often assumed that the purpose of inquiries is simply to postpone indefinitely difficult decisions such as this.

Chapter 7

Exercise 7.1

Here are five examples, one of each type. In each case, claim 1 is the conclusion, and the other claims are all dependent premises in one group.

Reasoning from cause

1   Cigarette smoking is the most significant cause of lung cancer.
2   Almost all people with lung cancer have been exposed to cigarette smoke.
3   Few lung cancer sufferers show any evidence that other causes are responsible for their disease.

Notice how the two premises establish the common element (smoking) and also assert that no other factor is usually involved.

Reasoning from generalisation

1   Giulio is not likely to live for much longer.
2   Giulio has lung cancer.
3   Very few lung cancer patients survive their disease for more than a year.

4   Giulio has been ill for over six months now.

Claim 3 acts as the framing premise, showing why Giulio's illness and its length lead to the given conclusion.

Reasoning from specific cases

1   Smoking should be banned in restaurants.
2   A recent representative survey of Australians found that most of them believed smoking should be banned in restaurants.
3   In a democratic country such as Australia, the wishes of the majority should be implemented.

Many arguments from specific cases establish factual claims, but (with the appropriate framing premise), they can also support an explicit value claim. Claim 2 is written as a summary of the survey subjects' views, representing the hundreds of individual opinions expressed in that survey.

Reasoning from analogy

1   Cigarette smoking that does not harm other people should not be banned.
2   Cigarettes and alcohol are similar in that they are addictive, potentially disease-causing substances.
3   Society condones the drinking of alcohol as long as it does not cause harm to other people.
4   It is good for societies to treat similar situations in a consistent manner.

The strength of this analogy depends on the similarity of drinking and smoking in relevant respects. Claim 2 seeks to establish this similarity, while claim 4 asserts that the similarity should be interpreted within a framework of consistency (normally we would 'leave out' this claim—see chapter 5 on implied premises).

Reasoning from terms

1   Cigarette smoke includes smoke inhaled both actively, from one's own smoking, and passively, from others' cigarettes.
2   Cigarette smoke can enter the lungs actively when a person is smoking.
3   Cigarette smoke can enter the lungs passively when a person is inhaling others' smoke.
4   Whichever way smoke enters the body, there is no qualitative difference in its effects on the lung.

This argument establishes a particular definition of 'cigarette smoke' (which might then be used to simplify another argument). The framework for this argument is provided by claim 4. Note that it is definitely not a causal argument: it is simply defining some term or concept.

Chapter 8

Exercise 8.1

At this stage, there is no 'answer'. However you might want to review and organise your list after having done exercise 8.3.

Exercise 8.2

Here are two further comments. First, learn how to 'read' effectively ('reading' includes watching, listening, observing, and so on). The 'knowledge' we want in those five classes will *not* have a label that tells us where it fits into this classification system. Rather, it is our own analysis, while we read, that begins to make these interconnections between classes of knowledge. Hence *active* reading—with a keen awareness of the possible outcomes, the questions to be answered, the extra questions that might emerge, and so on—is crucial.

Second, everyone is reasonably good at searching for the third of these four types (basic details and evidence), yet smart thinking is precisely about the way that evidence gathered in this search can be related to values, assumptions, other possible conclusions, and contexts. In that sense, we need to work hardest and learn most about the other types of information. Experience and study tend to throw up great masses of 'facts', data, or evidence, and the other three types of information get 'hidden' or 'lost'; learn to read through the detail to seek out the more general types of information.

Exercise 8.3

The point of the exercise is not to come to conclusions about the 'right answer' but to develop your conscious ability to ask questions about the sources of the information you are seeking. In other words, to be effective reasoners, we need to do more than ask 'What is in this book/experiment/article/interview that I can use in my argument?'; we must also ask questions such as:

- Why should I use this source?
- Can I trust this source?
- What sort of source is it: direct? indirect?
- Under what conditions was the information in this source produced?
- What was the original purpose of the source?
- What methods, approaches, or definitions does the source employ?
- Who is it being written for?
- Does it tell me more about the author or about the topic?
- When was it written or performed?
- How does the context of this source affect the information within it?

As noted at the start of chapter 8, good analysis is as much about asking questions as it is about finding answers. Hence, if our research is to be an active and effective part of our analysis, we need to think about the questions that will help us to understand our sources of information, as well as what they contain. Put simply, these questions help to reveal what lies in and behind the text, and to orient our research towards what we intend to do with the information once we have it.

Exercise 8.4

While we are usually more than capable of taking single claims and whole arguments or explanations from what we read, and probably are learning the art of coming away from research with more questions, the third and fourth categories are tricky. Summarising an entire piece of written work does *not* involve noting down individual bits and pieces ('key points', facts, main conclusions) but requires that you understand the entirety of the work and then, in your own words, write a short argument that sums up what the author is saying (perhaps using the analytical structure format). Identifying the assumptions and values that underlie a text is equally tricky and demands, at the very least, that you think carefully about the sorts of questions covered in exercise 8.3.

Chapter 9

Exercise 9.1

The main aim of this exercise is to make you think about the following crucial philosophical idea: how you study a topic (for example, the methods used, your definitions and founding assumptions about the nature of that topic, the way that the topic is 'isolated' from other possible topics, or other possible ways of studying the topic) will always influence the results you get. We tend to think that knowledge becomes objective when we put aside our personal biases, assumptions, and beliefs, and seek the truth in a 'disinterested' manner. However, the main external influence on our reasoning is not our emotions or subjective prejudices, but the in-built 'bias' of the methods and theories we use. Of course, that said, many disciplines (especially in the sciences) work from a different philosophical assumption: that the methods used are 'neutral', that they have no influence on the outcome of the research and analysis, and hence that knowledge is *not* intersubjective. Find out for yourself just what sort of philosophy of knowledge your 'discipline' or profession works within.

Exercise 9.2

The sorts of internal questions you might ask are, by and large, determined by the methodological, definitive, and theoretical frameworks in which you are operating. Moreover, because questions are always about the relationships between knowledge, any question you ask to find out information or knowledge will be based on something you already know. The trick to being a smart thinker is to know enough to be able to ask the right questions, but also to be prepared continually to adjust the questions you are asking and answering in light of the answers you come up with.

If you want further practice, develop the 'Olympic games' example that I have been using: begin with the claims that I have given you and expand on them.

Exercise 9.3

I will leave this one for you to work out. However, it might be worth reviewing chapters 5 and 6, which can assist you in considering the strengths and weaknesses of the argument. Once you know its weaknesses you can correct them; the strengths can, perhaps, be emphasised. If you want more practice, you can keep working through the 'Olympic games' example in a similar manner.

Glossary of Key Terms and Concepts

These 'key terms' summarise and draw together various points and concepts discussed in the text. Each includes a reference to the chapter in which they are first discussed; many are generally applicable throughout the book.

analogy, reasoning from

The conclusion is established by *comparing similarities* between like objects in the premises. The key questions to ask are about the similarities and differences between the known case and the case under discussion. (See chapter 7.)

analysis

The process of thinking through the connections and interrelations between individual 'bits' of information (be they facts, values, opinions, possibilities, predictions, or whatever). Arguing and explaining are about communicating your considered view of these connections (in relation to a particular topic). Analysis is the process of finding out about, thinking through, and reflecting upon the connections in preparation for communicating. Compare with *analytical questions* and *analytical structure*. (See chapter 8.)

analytical questions

Any questions designed to guide our research or reasoning by suggesting possible relations between claims. Questions can either relate primarily to our own text or to its connections with the surrounding context. (See chapter 8.)

analytical structure

The essential structure of claims and of the links between them, which lies behind the narrative expression of arguments and explanations, and which can be represented as

174

a list of claims and a diagram. The primary use of the analytical structure format is as a planning tool before or during writing and research. (See chapter 3.)

appeal to authority

A special form of reasoning in which a claim is supported by reference to an authority on that subject. Authority may stem from academic qualification, experience, or special knowledge, but in each case, the authority must be relevant to the claim being supported. References and footnotes are two of the most common forms in which we encounter appeals to authority. Theoretically, an appeal to authority is itself an argument that establishes the credentials of the authority and its relevance. However, in practice, it is an accepted convention simply to refer to the authority concerned. (See chapter 5.)

argument

Reasoning that seeks to establish the truth of a doubtful claim (which is its conclusion). It does not, in this context, mean a disagreement. But the process of arguing tends to involve assertions and counter-assertions. Arguments are required where the proposition claimed in the conclusion is in doubt or is presumed doubtful for 'argument's sake' (as we often say). An argument is not the same as a theme or topic: themes or topics are the broad areas of interest and investigation within which arguments (or explanations) occur. Compare with *explanation*. (See chapter 2.)

assumption

In relation to the particular structures of reasoning, any claim or link that is not explicitly expressed can be said to be implied or assumed. These implications are the result of our assuming that the claim or link is 'obvious'. Such assumptions impede our ability to think clearly about the possibility that we might be wrong, or that other connections or claims are involved. More generally, an assumption is any unconscious or unexamined idea in the context of reasoning. Compare with *context*. (See chapter 2.)

audience

In relation to reasoning, the 'audience' is that group of people who we wish to convince of the correctness of our argument or explanation. The expectations, understandings, and assumptions of audiences form part of the context of our reasoning and are central to decisions about the effectiveness of that reasoning. The audience should be thought of as consisting both of people and of the *knowledge* on which those people will draw when responding to our arguments and explanations. Compare with *context* and *subject*. (See chapter 2.)

breadth of reasoning

Good, effective arguments and explanations reason broadly, including a number of alternative and distinct 'reasons'. (See chapter 6.)

burden of proof

In any situation involving reasoning, we can discuss the degree of support needed for a conclusion to be acceptable in terms of the 'burden of proof' on the person presenting the argument or explanation. Burdens of proof are usually implied and contextual. (See chapter 6.)

casting

Casting is a process of looking at someone else's argument or explanation, in the narrative form, and then recovering from that form, an analytical structure which is done best by marking claims and traces of reasoning in the text, and then drawing a diagram to show the interlinkage of those claims. Casting is most usefully used as a way of building your understanding of reasoning, so that you can use the analytical structure format *from scratch* for your own arguments and explanations. (See chapter 3.)

cause, reasoning from

The conclusion proposes the relationship between cause and effect; the premises give evidence about the cause or causes and show why it is that the effect relates to that cause or causes. The key questions to ask in relation to reasoning from cause concern similarities and differences that might reveal the cause(s). Care is needed to avoid assuming a causal relationship when two events are simply coincidental or are *both* effects of an underlying cause. (See chapter 7.)

certainty

The measurement of probability involved in a claim; an important property in well-formed claims, useful in assessing the degree of support necessary for a particular conclusion. A conclusion and its premises are said to be 'coherent' in certainty when there is little variation in the measure of probability that all the claims make. The certainty component of a claim is often implicit but, in good reasoning, should be stated explicitly. Compare with *scope*. (See chapter 2.)

circular reasoning

A false form of reasoning in which the premise(s) appears to be different from the conclusion but which in fact is a restatement of that conclusion. You cannot reason for a claim by using the same claim again. (See chapter 4.)

claim

A claim is a statement that represents some event or idea about the way the world is or should be. It is distinguishable from other statements because, when considering a claim, it is possible to ask 'is this statement true or false?'. In relation to value claims, 'true or false' may be better expressed as 'sound or unsound'. (See chapter 2).

complex structure

Arguments and explanations are *complex* when they involve more than two layers of claims, that is, when they have premises that lead to a conclusion, and claims that establish the acceptability of those premises. A complex structure is built up from a series of overlapping simple structures. (See chapter 3.)

conclusion

In general terms, a claim that is being argued for or explained by the premises. The term 'conclusion' is only meaningful in relation to 'premise'. A conclusion can also be a premise to a further conclusion; these overlaps in function (claim as both premise and conclusion) can be seen in complex structures. Do not confuse with the more common use of 'conclusion' to mean 'the last part of an essay or presentation'. (See chapter 2.)

connotation

Words and statements have a denotative function (they denote or describe something), but they also carry with them varying connotations or hidden meanings about the objects and events they denote. Connotations do not spring from a word on its own but from the interrelations between words, and from the ways in which words are used and understood by authors and audiences. A text will always contain many connotations, which spring from the ways that audiences use their existing knowledge and expectations to interpret the words in the text. Obviously, if you and your audience share the same background or context, those connotations are less likely to cause misunderstandings. (See chapter 2.)

consistency

In an analogy, there is always a need to assess the degree of consistency between the like objects being compared or between the actions or ideas associated with those objects. Often, errors in analogies stem from assumptions of consistency that are not sustainable upon further analysis. (See chapter 7.)

context

The context in which reasoning takes place involves innumerable factors. They may include the audience (its knowledge, expectations, beliefs, relationship to the author of the reasoning), the conventional rules of presentation for particular knowledge groups, the goals authors are trying to achieve by reasoning, the other knowledge (assumptions, possible alternative arguments and explanations, and so on) that may bear upon our reasoning. Compare with *audience* and *assumption*. (See chapter 2.)

deduction

Deduction occurs only in those arguments where the premises implicitly outline a logical relationship that is expressed explicitly in the conclusion and where, if one accepts all the premises as true, one cannot then deny the conclusion. Essentially, this form of reasoning is simply a way of moving the key moment of proof from the final stage of the argument to the point where one is providing arguments in support of the premises. The opposite of *induction*. (See chapter 7.)

defining premise

A claim that, when serving as a premise, functions to define some term that is important to the whole argument. A defining premise must be used in a chain with other premises. Compare with *dependent premise*. (See chapter 4.)

dependent premise

Premises are said to be dependent when they form a chain that, when taken together, provides a reason for a conclusion. Unpacking a reason leads to the proper development of such chains. They should be grouped together above a horizontal line (_____) in the structure diagram. (See chapter 4.)

depth of reasoning

Arguments or explanations are deep when they explore all the subtleties of their reasons (unpacked into chains of dependent premises, possibly with further support for each of these premises). (See chapter 6.)

descriptive claim

A claim that describes without judging what is good or bad about the object being described. Descriptive claims that are completely free of value judgment are few in number because of the way in which all words, when written and read in context, can imply certain values. Values are often a significant aspect of the connotation that accompanies the obvious meanings of words or claims. Compare with *value claim*. (See chapter 2.)

effective reasoning

Effective reasoning does not necessarily guarantee that our conclusions will be proven correct or that the explanation for them will be accurate. However, consciously thinking about making our arguments and explanations more effective, first, provides us with a mental framework for better analysis and, second, ensures that, when we communicate with others, our reasoning is as convincing as it can be. (See chapters 5 and 6.)

exclamation

A statement that is exclaimed (that is, expressed with surprise or emotion). Many exclamations do not make statements that can be assessed as true or false, or as reasonable or unreasonable. Hence, many exclamations are not claims. (See chapter 2.)

explanation

A type of reasoning that seeks to explain, by means of premises, why a particular circumstance or idea has come about. (This idea or circumstance is reported in the conclusion.) Compare with *argument*. (See chapter 2.)

framing premise

A claim that, when serving as a premise, functions to establish why it is that the other premise(s) supports the conclusion. A framing premise must be used in a chain with other premises. Compare with *dependent premise*. (See chapter 4.)

generalisation, reasoning from

The conclusion is about a specific case; the premises show that the case fits some general category, and they state the particular property or consequence that pertains to all members of the general category. The key questions to ask about a particular case are: Does it fit this generalisation? And, if so, what general knowledge thereby applies to this case? (See chapter 7.)

implied premise

A premise not explicitly stated in an argument or explanation that, nevertheless, can be inferred by a reader as being necessary to make sense of the reasoning. Implied premises are often associated with the use of apparently *independent premises*. Compare with *assumption*. (See chapter 5.)

independent premise

A single premise that expresses a reason for a conclusion on its own. An independent premise is likely to be a sign that there are implied dependent premises. (See chapter 4.)

induction

Reasoning in which the conclusion may be more or less likely if the premises are true but which is not conclusively guaranteed even if all the premises are true. We see induction in arguments that depend on the observation and reporting of real-world events which, by their nature, can never be certain. The opposite of *deduction*. (See chapter 7.)

information

Information is often thought to be a more disorganised, unprocessed version of knowledge. Information is a collection of claims; knowledge is that information processed and interrelated. In this book, knowledge and information are used interchangeably, but the basic idea that reasoning enables us to organise what we know is still important. Compare with *knowledge*. (See chapters 8 and 9.)

internal connection (within a claim)

The key property of claims that allows them to be used in reasoning to express complex ideas. Internal connections provide the basis for the external links between claims. Compare with *dependent premise*. (See chapter 2.)

intersubjective

Knowledge is said to be intersubjective when the decisions about the 'truth' of claims and claim relationships are made by 'subjects' (that is, people)—in this case the authors and audiences of reasoning. Compare with *objective* and *subject*. (See chapter 9.)

knowledge

Knowledge (which we might also call information) is the 'stuff' of reasoning. Knowledge is always relational. First, knowledge is about claims and the links between them. Second, knowledge is created and maintained intersubjectively, that is, between audiences and authors. Classes of knowledge and types of information (see chapter 8) are ways of thinking about the generic relations of knowledge to our particular topic when researching. Compare with *objective*. (See chapters 8 and 9.)

link words

The traces to be found in natural language of the mental processes of reasoning; a useful but unreliable guide to the exact connections between claims. (See chapter 3.)

list of claims

One half of the analytical structure format. A list of claims shows clearly the claims to which the diagram of interrelationships refers. Compare with *structure diagram*. (See chapter 3.)

mind-map

A tool that assists in analysing connections, concepts, and so on. A mind-map is not an analytical structure format because the ideas and links are written down in a tentative way, simply as a way of 'externalising' unprocessed information. (See chapter 9.)

modes of analysis

Direct analysis concerns, as much as possible, the particular topic of an argument or explanation. Indirect analysis concerns what others think and write about that topic. Hypothetical analysis involves the explicit consideration of possible (rather than actual) situations and the open discussion of assumptions. All three modes are interrelated and are usually used in concert. For example, if I were to discuss the way people write about reasoning, that would be direct; if I then considered philosophical arguments about the way people write about reasoning, that would be indirect. Compare with *source*. (See chapter 5.)

narrative flow

The written or spoken expression of reasoning in which the analytical structure is turned into natural language. In narrative flow, we find traces of the linking process, as well as claims that have been reorganised to meet the requirements of good expression. As a result, it can be hard to see what is going on in reasoning unless we also think about the analytical structure that lies behind the narrative. Compare with *analytical structure*. (See chapter 3.)

narrative sequence plan

A plan for writing or presenting in which ideas are listed in the same order that they will appear on the written page or in the presentation. The links between the ideas are, thus, indications of the flow (rather than the analytical structure). Such a plan is useful because it 'externalises' the order in a way that allows you to check it and revise it. (See chapter 9.)

objective

Some philosophers regard knowledge and judgments as objective when they appear to relate solely to the object that they make claims about (which may be a thing, event, circumstance, or whatever). An objective claim is usually considered to be a 'true' claim. Other philosophers argue that no claim can ever be solely about the object since language is an intersubjective medium, full of connotations and hidden implications, which make it impossible to be objective. According to this view, the 'truth' of claims is settled intersubjectively, through a complex process of social interaction that draws in part on objective knowledge but is different from it. Compare with *knowledge*. (See chapter 9.)

order

A type of statement that is not a claim but that demands obedience from its audience. (See chapter 2.)

premise

In general terms, a claim that is used to argue for or explain another claim (the conclusion). The term 'premise' is only meaningful in relation to a *conclusion*. (See chapter 2.)

propositional logic

Occurs when an if/then statement (or its differently worded equivalent) is used to propose, in the premises, a relationship between two states of affairs, or events, or matters; normally the other premise in such arguments is the 'if' component of the proposition, permitting the 'then' component to be the conclusion. Often associated with deductive reasoning. (See chapter 7.)

purposes of reasoning

The purposes of reasoning are what arguments and explanations seek to achieve. Arguments predict future events, establish what is or was the case, or show why a certain action should occur. Explanations explain why something happened or is happening, or they justify why someone did something. (See chapter 2.)

question

A type of statement that is not a claim but that genuinely seeks information. A question can imply some relationship. Compare with *analytical questions*. (See chapter 2.)

reason

Used loosely, this term describes the information that supports or explains a particular conclusion. As used in this book, a 'reason' is an initial statement of why a particular conclusion is acceptable—a reason that must then be 'unpacked' or expanded into a chain of premises in order to give appropriate depth to our reasoning. (See chapter 4.)

relativism

A short-hand term for the idea that knowledge is not to be judged 'true or false' by comparing it to the real world, but instead by reference to the humans who hold that knowledge. Extreme relativism, in which 'everyone's opinion is as good as anyone else's opinion' (subjective knowledge), is the opposite of the anti-relativist position of objective knowledge. In neither case is the social aspect of reasoning properly thought through. Smart thinking is primarily concerned with *social relativism*, in which knowledge is constructed intersubjectively. Compare with *intersubjective* and *knowledge*. (See chapter 9; see also chapter 1.)

relevance

Premises are relevant to a conclusion if they provide some basis on which to accept that conclusion. We can say that, if true, a relevant premise makes the conclusion more likely. Relevance is involved in reasoning in many ways. For example, appeals to authority require the use of relevant authorities; reasoning from analogy requires that comparisons be made between relevantly similar cases; reasoning from generalisation requires that the relevance of the generalisation to the specific case be established. Crucially, a framing premise is often used explicitly to establish just how premises relate to a conclusion. (See chapter 6.)

scope

The extent or coverage of a claim; an important property in terms of writing well-formed claims and assessing the degree of support necessary for a particular conclusion. A conclusion and its premises are said to be 'coherent' in scope when there is little variation in the way that the claims report the extent of their information. The scope component of a claim is often implicit but, in good reasoning, should be stated explicitly. Compare with *certainty*. (See chapter 2.)

self-evident claim

A self-evident claim is one that, relative to the audience and context in which it is presented, requires no foundation or, literally, is so obviously acceptable that it provides its own evidence of acceptability. What is self-evident for one group or individual, or in one context, may not be self-evident in other situations. Compare with *well-founded claim*. (See chapter 5.)

simple structure

An argument or explanation is said to be simple when it involves only two layers of claims: the premises and the conclusion. No matter how many premises are offered, no matter how many distinct groups of dependent premises there are, such arguments are not complex. Compare with *complex structure*. (See chapter 3.)

source

Sources can be either direct (primary) or indirect (secondary). The difference between them is usually contextual, but generally speaking, direct sources relate to the topic of our reasoning; indirect sources relate to what others have reasoned about our topic. Obviously, if the topic of our argument or explanation is what others have written or said, then what appears to be an indirect source can in fact be direct. (See chapter 8.)

specific cases, reasoning from

The conclusion generalises beyond the scope of the specific cases in the premises; the premises give the evidence regarding those cases. The key question to ask is: do these cases give rise to some reliable generalisation that applies to all of them or all like cases? (See chapter 7.)

statement

The generic name for an ordered, meaningful group of words. Statements may or may not be claims. A statement is not a sentence: 'sentence' is a term used to describe the narrative flow of words; statement is a term to denote the analytical units that make up reasoning. Compare with *claim*. (See chapter 2.)

strength of support

Even acceptable and relevant premises do not always provide sufficient support to show or explain their conclusions. Judgments of the necessary strength of support needed in reasoning are difficult, since they depend largely on the context in which that reasoning is taking place. Compare with *burden of proof*. (See chapter 6.)

structure diagram

One half of the analytical structure format. A structure diagram shows the interrelationship of claims in a standardised way. It is distinguished from the arrangement of claims in narrative flow by the fact that, in a diagram, the conclusion is always last and the order of claims above it indicates the 'steps' we need to take to reach that conclusion from our starting point. The key elements are the [↓] symbol, to show premise–conclusion links; the + symbol, to show premise–premise links; and the use of horizontal lines (_____), to show grouped chains of premises. (See chapter 3.)

sub-argument

Any one component layer of a complex argument. For example, consider an argument structure in which claims 2 and 3 support claim 4, which in turn joins with claim 5 to support the conclusion—claim 1. The main argument concerns claim 1 and so the sub-argument consists in the structure 2+3 [↓] 4. (See chapter 3.)

subject

The term 'subject' is used in many different ways in English. Used loosely, it can mean the topic one is investigating, as in 'the subject of my paper is the continued inequalities of patriarchal culture'. In grammar, 'subject' refers to the part of a sentence with which the verb agrees: 'domestic violence [subject] remains rife in our society [object]'. However, in this book, subject is used to refer to a thinking, conscious person (so that authors and audiences of reasoning are 'human subjects'). Its meaning only becomes clear in relation to the term 'object'—those events, ideas, things in the world about which we (as subjects) make claims. For example, some philosophers might argue that the difference between 'subjective' and 'objective' analysis is that the former involves the desires and biases of the subject doing the analysis, whereas the latter is uninfluenced, except by the true nature of the object. However, it can also be argued that knowledge and reasoning (whatever their objective elements) always involve people and so can be regarded as 'inter-subjective'. The human subjects bringing about this intersubjectivity are not merely 'people' but include the knowledge, ideas, structures, and attitudes that make those people who they are. (See chapters 2 and 9.)

sweeping generalisation

A mistake in reasoning that occurs when the scope or certainty of the conclusion is inconsistent with (normally much greater than) the scope or certainty of the premises that support it. (See chapter 4.)

terms, reasoning from

The conclusion proposes a particular definition based on the terms laid out in the premises. The key question is: how can I express my definition in terms that make clear its meaning in a particular context? (See chapter 7.)

text

We call any connected series of statements a text. Texts are only meaningful in context, which is literally all the potential knowledge and audiences that go along *with* a text. Compare with *context*. (See chapter 2.)

value claim

Many claims have a value component. Some are explicit; others are implicit, buried in the particular choice of words. Often a claim that is (in itself) descriptive takes on a value element from other claims to which it is connected. Remember, too, that in such situations different authors and audiences can invest the same claim with different values. Compare with *descriptive claim*. (See chapter 2.)

well-formed claim

A claim is well formed when it clearly expresses what its author intends it to say. Good formation of claims requires authors to consider consciously properties of connections and issues of value, scope, and certainty. A well-formed claim may or may not be true, but at least its clarity allows us to assess its truth. While, no matter how hard we try, we can never be sure our audience will always understand exactly what we mean, writing well-formed claims ensures that at least we know what we are trying to say. Compare with *connotation*. (See chapter 5.)

well-founded claim

A claim is well founded if, relative to the audience and context in which it is presented, it is likely to be accepted as true. Well-founded claims often depend on appeals to authority or a complete argument or explanation to ensure that their truth is less open to doubt. Compare with *self-evident claim*. (See chapter 5.)

word

The basic unit from which we construct statements. Words are only meaningful in relation to other words. Compare with *connotation*. (See chapter 2.)

Further Reading

Further reading on knowledge and philosophy

Doyal, Len and Harris, Ken, *Empiricism, Explanation and Rationality in the Social Sciences*, Routledge and Kegan Paul, London, 1986.
    A very comprehensive treatment of the topic. The authors' main argument is that naive empiricism (that is, the belief that facts are facts and we find them) is wrong because all 'facts' are interpretive claims based in political and/or social circumstances.

Gaarder, Jostein, *Sophie's World: A Novel about the History of Philosophy*, Phoenix House, London, 1995.
    A story about a teenage girl who is drawn into a mystery that involves an unseen philosophy teacher who sends her short commentaries on philosophy. The plot is excellent, and the philosophy 'lessons' are not bad either.

Gellner, Ernest, *Reason and Culture*, Blackwell, Oxford, 1992.
    A broad-brush history of the development of modern 'Reason', pointing to the ways in which knowledge and knowledge systems (such as reasoning) are non-objective.

Kuhn, Thomas, *The Structure of Scientific Revolutions*, University of Chicago Press, Chicago, 1970.
    A revolutionary book in itself. It argues for the centrality of non-objective theoretical paradigms and for the cultural practices of scientists in determining 'facts'.

Lloyd, Genevieve, *The Man of Reason*, Methuen, London, 1984.
    Much Western philosophy (the basis of this book) is gender-biased, both in its practical exclusion of women and also in its founding ideas. Lloyd gives a very readable account of the ways in which the social context of patriarchy (men in charge) has influenced the 'objective' ideas of philosophy.

McCarthy, E. Doyle, *Knowledge as Culture: The New Sociology of Knowledge*, Routledge, London, 1996.

Excellent introduction to, and then extended discussion of, the way that social and cultural theorists have developed more sophisticated understandings of 'knowledge' as a product of social and cultural forces in the past fifty years.

Morton, Adam, *Philosophy in Practice*, Blackwell, Oxford, 1996.
Covers many issues relating to both epistemology and other aspects of philosophy (such as identity, ethics, and so on); particularly useful for its discussions of certainty and doubt.

Schirato, Tony and Yell, Susan, *Communication and Culture: An Introduction*, Sage, London, 2000.
A very comprehensive treatment of the way meaning is generated by context, intertextuality, and discourse within culture and society. This book, unlike many critical thinking texts, is grounded in the insights of post-structuralist philosophy and will significantly assist your understanding of the way 'objective' truth is a construct of social processes as much as it is a property of objects in the world.

Stefik, Mark, *Internet Dreams: Archetypes, Myths, and Metaphors*, MIT Press, Cambridge, Mass., 1996.
An eclectic collection of primary and secondary analysis of the early days of the Internet. Used here for the work of Licklider but an interesting commentary on why technologies of information and communication do not substitute for reasoning in our search for information.

Further reading on reasoning

Bowell, Tracy and Kemp, Gary, *Critical Thinking: A Concise Guide*, Routledge, London, 2002.
Alternative book to the larger reasoning textbooks listed below: good concise explanations and advice.

Browne, M. Neil and Keeley, Stuart M., *Asking the Right Questions: A Guide to Critical Thinking*, Prentice-Hall, Englewood Cliffs, NJ, 2003 (7th edn).
An excellent book that organises its ideas around the key concept of analytical questioning, which I deploy in chapters 8 and 9.

Cederblom, Jerry and Paulsen, David W., *Critical Reasoning*, Wadsworth, Belmont, CA, 2000 (5th edn).
A large reasoning textbook that contains an excellent discussion of the problems and advantages of relying on experts and authorities.

Dowden, Bradley H., *Logical Reasoning*, Wadsworth, Belmont, CA, 1998.
Another textbook with a particularly good chapter on explanations and on causal reasoning.

Little, J. Frederick, Groarke, Leo A., and Tindale, Christopher W., *Good*

Reasoning Matters! A Constructive Approach to Critical Thinking, McClelland & Stewart, Toronto, 1989.

This book was, in part, responsible for my emphasis on writing arguments and explanations, rather than analysing them. Its advice on writing good arguments is particularly helpful.

Makau, Josina M., *Reasoning and Communication: Thinking Critically about Arguments*, Wadsworth, Belmont, CA, 1990.

A shorter work, with less emphasis on methods (such as casting). It is particularly useful for its discussion of the contexts in which argumentation takes place; a new edition was published in 1998.

Nickerson, Raymond S., *Reflections On Reasoning*, Lawrence Erlbaum, Hillsdale, NJ, 1986.

This book provides some very revealing insights into the processes of teaching and learning the skills of reasoning.

Rudinow, Joel and Barry, Vincent, *Invitation to Critical Thinking*, Wadsworth, Belmont, CA, 2003 (5th edn).

Contains an excellent section on casting and a comprehensive discussion of the generic errors that people make in reasoning.

Ruggiero, Vincent Ryan, *Beyond Feelings: A Guide to Critical Thinking*, Mayfield, Mountainview, CA, 1984.

A much republished book that provides simple, common-sense advice on many issues related to reasoning; it also provides an excellent example of how the failure to consider contextual issues can render much of this advice impractical.

Ruggiero, Vincent Ryan, *The Art of Thinking: A Guide to Critical and Creative Thought*, Pearson Longman, 2000 (6th edn).

More up-to-date work by Ruggiero that expands on the original guide in a more 'textbook' manner. Of value is the focus the author places on personal change and commitment to critical thinking, instead of simple technique.

Rybacki, Karyn C. and Rybacki, Donald J., *Advocacy and Opposition: An Introduction to Argumentation*, Prentice-Hall, Englewood Cliffs, NJ, 1986.

This work gives considerable advice on the process of proving particular types of conclusions and inspired my approach in chapter 8.

Toulmin, Stephen, *The Uses of Argument*, Cambridge University Press, Cambridge, 2003.

Most recent book by Toulmin, one of the most influential analysts of critical thinking and argumentation.

Toulmin, Stephen, Rieke, Richard, and Janik, Allan, *An Introduction to Reasoning*, Macmillan, New York, 1984.

An excellent, thorough critical thinking textbook, with a particular emphasis on the different ways in which premises and premise-like statements combine to demonstrate a conclusion. My concept of 'framing premises' was developed from Toulmin's much more complex discussion of the 'warrants' and 'backgrounds' that are involved in argumentation. This book is useful, also, for its recognition of the need for a contextualised approach to critical thinking.

Waller, Bruce N., *Critical Thinking: Consider your Verdict*, Prentice-Hall, Englewood Cliffs, NJ, 2000 (4th edn).

Although this book concentrates on the role of critical thinking in the decisions made by juries (and thus draws most of its examples from the legal context), it provides particularly sensible discussions of relevance and assumptions.

Further reading on writing and communicating

Hay, Iain, Bochner, Diane, and Dungey, Carol, *Making the Grade*, OUP, Melbourne, 2002.

Wide-ranging and up-to-date advice on study skills, including assistance with writing and communicating.

Murphy, Eamon, *You Can Write: A Do-it-Yourself Manual*, Longman, Melbourne, 1985.

Excellent advice on writing and the use of plans; still useful twenty years after publication because of its clear tone and style.

Summers, Jane and Brett Smith (eds), *Communication Skills Handbook: How to Succeed in Written and Oral Communication*, Milton, Qld, John Wiley, 2002.

Covers many different aspects of communication, with a particular emphasis on business communication.

Guide to Important Skills

Use the following questions and answers as an index to specific advice in *Smart Thinking* on the key skills of reasoning. They are designed to help you 'get back into' the book after you have read it thoroughly for the first time; they also provide a basic summary of what *Smart Thinking* can do to 'smarten up' your own thinking. These questions provide a connection between the skills discussed in this book and the most common concerns that people have when faced with the task of writing an essay or report, or preparing an oral presentation. In other words, these questions show you how to understand and apply smart-thinking skills in practical contexts.

Each question is answered in brief, and then page references are given to direct you to the detailed advice necessary for you to answer the question for yourself. The guide is divided into two sections. The first contains questions that are more general and that are expressed without mentioning specific concepts from the book (the answers then give those concepts); the key issue in each of these questions is presented in bold type. The second section contains questions that guide you towards specific concepts that are mentioned in the book (in bold). If you have not yet read *Smart Thinking* through thoroughly, you should begin with the first section.

General questions

How can I think through **complex ideas** so that I have a good understanding of them?
Ask questions, do not be satisfied with easy answers, and do not make assumptions about what things mean. (See pp 83–6, 105–7, 124–8.)

What do I need to do to be **convincing** in my reports, essays, and presentations?
Make sure you have a good analytical structure and have a strong argument or explanation. (See pp 81–6, 121–8.)

190

How do I make my reasoning **easy to follow** for people reading or listening to my arguments and explanations?
Make sure that you properly indicate the reasoned links you are making, signalling the analytical structure to your audience. (See pp 27–9.)

Why, and how, should I use **footnotes or other references** in my work?
They provide references to authority, which strengthen the substance of your reasoning. (See pp 65–7, 78–9.)

What should be the **goal of my reasoning**?
Reasoning has many purposes, each of which will affect the precise way that you argue or explain. (See pp 4, 21–2, 124–5.)

When writing or presenting, how do I deal with **ideas with which I do not agree**?
Make sure you use reasoning to show explicitly why an idea is wrong, thereby preventing criticism of your work. (See pp 85–6, 112–13.)

How do I make sure that I understand the **interpretive frameworks** that are central to all knowledge?
In your thinking, you need to distinguish between 'facts' and the way that they can be understood as relating to other 'facts'; in your writing, make sure that you use framing premises. (See pp 5–6, 45–6, 78, 111–13.)

What are the two **key components** of a good argument or explanation?
You need premises (reasons, evidence) to support your conclusion (a clear statement of what you are arguing for or explaining). (See pp 19–22, 32–6.)

How can I distinguish between *my* ideas and what I am saying about *others'* ideas in my essays and presentations?
Clearly distinguish between when you are arguing directly and when you are arguing indirectly. (See pp 57–60, 112–16.)

What is wrong with giving just **one reason** for my conclusion?
Your arguments will not have enough breadth and will not address all the issues that your audience is expecting you to consider. (See pp 44–5, 71–4.)

How can I be more effective in doing **research and reading** before I write?
Ask questions, and understand the relationship between your sources and your own essay, presentation, or report. (See pp 107–13.)

How can I assess **someone else's reasoning** to see if they have presented a good argument or explanation?
You can 'cast' their work into claims and a structure diagram. (See pp 12–15, 32–7.)

Specific questions

How do I use **analogies**?
By comparing items and drawing conclusions based on their similarities. (See pp 99–100.)

How do I avoid making **assumptions** in my essays, presentations, and reports?
Do not take the truth of a claim—or its relationship with other claims—for granted; stop and think about what your audiences expect you to do and what they already know. (See pp 7, 11–12, 73–4, 122–7.)

How can I begin to understand the **audiences** of my arguments and explanations?
Regard your audiences as having certain expectations about what you should say to them and how you should say it, as well as certain background knowledge that directly affects your reasoning. (See pp 63–4, 73–4, 81–6, 122–7.)

What is **casting**?
Casting is a process of recovering the analytical structure from another author's narrative. (See pp 32–4, 135–49.)

How do I write about **causes** and **effects**?
Reasoning from cause requires you to use premises that state the cause(s) of an effect that is expressed in the conclusion. (See pp 95–6, 110.)

What do I need to know about **claims** in order to use them effectively in planning my reports, essays, and presentations?
You must attend to their key properties and express them precisely. (See pp 11–14, 57–61, 86–7.)

How do I plan **complex** argument structures?
A complex argument structure is just a series of overlapping, intertwined simple arguments. (See pp 36–8, 53–4, 65–8, 71–4.)

Why is **context** so important in reasoning effectively?
No argument or explanation (text) is ever written or read in isolation: background (or context)—which includes the expectations, assumptions, and implied concepts of both author and audience—always affects the text. (See pp 11–12, 81–6, 122–4.)

How do I go about using **definitions** in my work?
Make sure that your definitions are clear and are integrated in the main structure of your reasoning. (See pp 47–8, 57–8, 100.)

How do I make sure that my essays and presentations go into enough **depth** to be convincing?
Make sure that you expand the reasons for your conclusion so that they are comprehensive and form a chain of dependent premises. (See pp 40–5, 71–4.)

How are **knowledge** and reasoning connected?
They are two aspects of the same whole: knowledge is expressed and learnt as reasoning; reasoning utilises and relies on knowledge. (See pp 104–6, 109–13.)

How would I define **reasoning**, and what can it do for me?
Reasoning is about the relationships between ideas and events; using it helps you to think smart and communicate effectively. (See pp 1–9.)

How can I make sure that I am being **relevant**?
Make sure that your premises really do say something that supports your conclusion and that your audience understands this connection. (See pp 75–80.)

What do I need to know if I want to use **specific cases** and **general rules** in my arguments?
You need to understand the way in which general conclusions can flow from specific cases and how general rules provide the framework for establishing specific conclusions. (See pp 96–9, 108.)

How can I improve the **structure** and **logic** of my essays, reports, and presentations?
Use the analytical structure format to plan your work before you begin writing. (See pp 34–6, 128–32.)

Why is the **truth** (or falsity) of claims so important?
All arguments and explanations are designed to establish the truth of one claim on the basis of other true claims. (See pp 12–13, 61–7.)